Diamond Bessie
& The Shepherds

PUBLICATIONS OF THE TEXAS FOLKLORE SOCIETY NUMBER XXXVI

Diamond Bessie & The Shepherds

Edited By Wilson M. Hudson

1972
THE ENCINO PRESS
AUSTIN

FIRST EDITION

© 1972 : Texas Folklore Society : Austin
Published by The Encino Press : 2003 South Lamar : Austin
Design : William D. Wittliff

Foreword

THIS
is a miscellany of the kind that our Publications have made familiar
to readers interested in folklore. The title refers to the first two
articles, which deal with two folk dramas, one secular and the other
religious. James W. Byrd describes the annual reenactment of a
famous murder trial at Jefferson, and John Igo draws out Julia
Nott Waugh on *Los Pastores* (*The Shepherds*) as it is presented in
San Antonio. The Spanish-religious theme is continued by Charles
B. Martin, who takes us to Seville for the celebration of Holy Week
in the old country.

E. J. Rissmann recalls the days when cotton was the farmer's
cash crop and every rural community had a gin that hummed from
daylight to dark in cotton-picking time. In the same area that Rissmann has in mind, Sara Clark describes graves decorated with seashells and inquires into the antiquity and significance of this practice. Moving just to the west of Rissmann's home ground, Esther
L. Mueller explains how the Sunday houses of Fredericksburg came
into existence and played a part in the lives of the German farmers
roundabout until good roads and automobiles made them unnecessary. Sylvia Grider makes us understand what a real dust storm in
the Panhandle was like back in 1935. Such storms were more in-

tense near their point of origin, but they still almost smothered the land as they rolled southeast and carried out to sea.

Next there is a run of four essays dealing with popular and sophisticated literature from the point of view of the folklorist. In the Old Southwest the camp meeting was for a while a religious gathering that drew thousands and plunged them into frenzies and seizures; naturally, as Bill F. Fowler shows, camp meetings were easy prey for certain humorists. O. Henry's treatment of politics and politicians is tinged with folk humor, as is made apparent by E. Hudson Long in his article. Kyra Jones delves into the question of the presence and function of myth in *The Winter of Our Discontent,* Steinbeck's last novel. Ann Miller Carpenter surveys American folk song from 1865 to 1920 to discover what aspects of railroading attracted the singers' attention and to estimate the impact of the railroad on American life.

James T. Bratcher and J. T. McCullen each deal with the pattern of an anecdote. The anecdote of the professor who didn't get in his grades is readily transferable from one campus to another in America, and Mr. Bratcher produces a version from England that harmonizes with the English way of rating students. The anecdote studied by Mr. McCullen has had a long history and a wide dissemination. To Arabs and Europeans it has seemed just that something insubstantial should be paid for by something equally insubstantial.

This book concludes with studies by two of our members who observed folk customs and dances in the far places of the world. While she was teaching in Greece, Pina S. Sturdivant took time to find out how marriages were made and celebrated in Thessaly and Macedonia. When Martin S. Shockley was in South Africa on a Fulbright Fellowship, he saw the workers in the Johannesburg mines dance on Sunday.

All in all, there is range and richness in what is offered here.

The time has come for me to say good-bye as secretary and editor for the Society. In the summer of 1951, while Mody Boatright was teaching in California, he asked me to edit *The Healer of Los Olmos*, and I did so. When he returned he invited me to join him and Allen Maxwell of SMU Press in preparing our annual volumes. Upon Mody's retirement in 1964 I was chosen to succeed him as secretary and editor. I have tried to carry on in his spirit and in the spirit of his predecessors, J. Frank Dobie and Stith Thompson. In the span from 1951 to 1971 I have edited or assisted in editing thirteen Publications for the Society, and I have edited the five books in the Paisano series. A translation of five Irish folktales, neither a Publication nor a Paisano, which I am now seeing through the press for the Society, will carry no designation of editor. Because I wanted to complete some books and projects of my own, in the spring of 1971 I asked to be relieved of my duties. It seemed to me that I had served my turn. At our last meeting, Francis E. Abernethy of Stephen F. Austin State University at Nacogdoches was elected secretary-editor. I hereby surrender to him, most willingly and confidently, these offices. He will know how to make the most of the ability and vitality inherent in the Texas Folklore Society, which has flourished since its foundation in 1909 and will continue to flourish for many a year.

WILSON M. HUDSON

Austin, Texas
September 17, 1971

Contents

Diamond Bessie
& The Shepherds

A Texas Folk Drama:
"The Diamond Bessie Murder Trial"

By JAMES W. BYRD

IN 1836 the townsites of Houston and Jefferson were established on the banks of two bayous in Texas. Houston, the largest of Southern ports today, was founded on Buffalo Bayou, and Jefferson, more important as a center of trade and commerce during the days before and following the Civil War, was located on Cypress Bayou of Caddo Lake.[1]

Although today Jefferson has a population of 3,000, in the 1870's it was a city with a population of 30,000. It was the trading point of East Texas; all roads led to Jefferson. The reason is clear. A natural barrier in Red River backed water into Cypress Bayou to an extent that navigation was possible as far inland as Jefferson, and steamboats landed there from New Orleans. Its river traffic began as early as 1845, and it was ahead of Shreveport as a focal point of navigation on Red River. At one time, Jefferson ranked as the largest city of the state, or, perhaps, second only to Galveston, according to which historian you read.

The Baptists must have been weak there, for the town was wide open with gambling, saloons, cockfight pits, and race tracks. In the 1860's and '70's, luxury river boats brought U. S. Presidents Ulysses S. Grant and Rutherford B. Hayes; financier Jay Gould; writers

3

Oscar Wilde and Walt Whitman; and actor Maurice Barrymore, the father of John, Ethel, and Lionel.

To this "Queen City of the Cypress," the center of commerce and culture, came hundreds of lesser known visitors, including one Abe Rothschild and his apparent bride, Bessie, dressed in fashionable clothes, wearing many diamonds. They registered at one of the good hotels[2] as "A. Monroe and wife" on January 18, 1877. At the end of three days, the couple went to an unusual midwinter picnic in the woods on January 21, 1877, and two weeks later the body of Bessie was found in the woods shot through the head. A Negro woman found her on February 5 while picking up firewood. Though murder was not rare in Jefferson, this one shocked that city and rocked the great state of Texas. Abe was tried for murder—three times.

So much is history, but what is history to a folklorist of the "folk"? According to George Orwell in his novel *1984*, "Past events have no objective existence, but survive only in written records and human memories." Folklorists and historians accept this dictum in principle; but historians emphasize the written records and folklorists emphasize the human memories. It has been said that the human mind preserves the memory of rituals, of dreams, of responses to the environment, but it forgets events. Folklore, in that case, is the last place one should go in search of "true" history. Conversely, history without folklore is dull. For example, more than half of the "facts" we remember about Washington and Lincoln—or even Lyndon B. Johnson—are folk anecdotes. We should acknowledge that local pride, prejudice, and passions play their part in the folklorization of history.[3]

One of the multiple definitions of folklore is "oral tradition in periodic contact with a more complex, literate society." Folk tradition does strange things to history; it changes dates, places, and names to suit the contemporary speaker or writer. Tradition often replaces history. "Tradition," Américo Paredes has said, "remembers but not as history remembers"; it builds "its own timeless world out of the wreck of history." That is one way to find history in folklore—in a state of wreck. Some interesting things can be done with the pieces. A folk drama in Texas furnishes a good example of how tradition replaces factual history.

"The Diamond Bessie Murder Trial" is presented annually in Jefferson as a part of a historical pilgrimage primarily designed to view the ante-bellum homes of the area. I went to see the play expecting to see a reenactment of a historical trial. It turned out to be the most authentic folk drama now produced annually in Texas.

The characters are played by the townspeople. Attorneys of Jefferson take the roles of prosecutor and defender; they know the historic case and improvise lines that suit them and the sense of humor of the audience. The plot is based not on history but on what "they say" and what "they" have been saying for years, i.e., folk beliefs. Abe Rothschild, the murderous villain, was a rich Jew[4] who could hire the best legal talent, including the then Congressman of the Jefferson district. Abe is shown as a handsome, cocksure scoundrel from the North. He wears an eye patch, like a Hathaway shirt ad, because he once attempted to commit suicide while pursued by the Jefferson law officers, and only managed to shoot out one eye.

"Diamond Bessie," or Bessie Stone, who appears only as a ghost in the drama, is portrayed as a beautiful girl betrayed by her innocence. She is evidently white, Anglo-Saxon, and Protestant, called, for short today, a WASP. One gets the impression she might be from Tara or some impressive Georgia plantation that produces such Southern Belles.

The court record itself is fantastic enough, but the play does not use much of it. The first trial in Jefferson resulted in a hung jury. When the venue was changed to Harrison County, Rothschild was sentenced to death. On December 30, 1879, a judgment was pronounced. Ironically, it stated that the defendant be "condemned to be hanged by the neck until he is dead and *that he pay the cost of this prosecution.*"[5] The legend is that the foreman of this jury drew a picture of a noose on the wall and said, "That is our verdict."

The verdict was reversed and the next trial was returned to Jefferson. Rothschild spent seven years in jail in Marshall without bail (about an average sentence for murder in Texas). His third and last trial was in Jefferson, which now had Jay Gould's railroad as well as the more romantic river boats. On the last day of the trial, the jury delayed until the morning northbound train blew its whistle while entering Jefferson. Then it returned a "not guilty" verdict. Rothschild leaped into a waiting carriage and was taken immediately to the train, whose conductor had agreed to wait for him.

At least that is the legend, firmly believed then and now. Repeating an even stronger legend, Jefferson people also affirm that $1,000 bills were handed down through a trap door in the ceiling of the jury room and that a grand piano was shortly to be seen at the residence of each juror.

In Jefferson, I saw the script for the play—such as it is.[6] It is only a rough outline, with a minimum of lines written out. Mostly the actors of each year improvise lines, based on the "memory" of the famous trial and the preceeding year's production of the play.

Scene I is in the Jefferson graveyard. Before a tombstone with the name Bessie Moore etched within a diamond-shaped diagram, a handsome stranger is kneeling to place red roses on the grave. He wears a dark suit, flowing black cape, and a black eye patch.

The eye patch is a complete give-away. This is Abe Rothschild, who, tradition says, often returned "in the dead of night" to put roses on Bessie's tomb. They were always mysteriously there the next morning, according to the caretaker of the cemetery, who in the play explains the tableau to a teen-aged helper.

The tombstone itself also mysteriously appeared. For twenty years it was believed that Abe put it there also in the dead of night; then a local stonecutter admitted before he died that he and a friend put it there as a joke. It is still there, but the play uses the legend rather than the later confession.[7]

Bessie appears in the first scene as a beautiful and lively ghost, dressed in a red velvet cloak, wearing many diamonds, as she was last seen alive, according to tradition.[8] Last summer a caretaker showed me her grave. The tombstone was still there, the sign put up by the Jessie Allen Wise Garden Club had been stolen by teenagers, and some white lace lingerie was hanging on the wrought-iron fence, indicating that Bessie must be a very lively ghost indeed.

Diamond Bessie appears again as a ghost in Scene II, in the anteroom of the courtroom. The building in which the play is staged was originally the Jewish Synagogue, and it makes a suitably historical setting for the drama.

The atmosphere is set by the words of a white-coated "darky" who dusts the courtroom while "a muttering crowd" is outside.

He observes, "I'd sho hate to be in dat white man's shoes . . . 'specially efin dat crowd ebber gets loose."

Abe, sitting alone in the anteroom, observes aloud: "But why am I so worried? I can't be convicted, the plans have been too well laid . . . ."

Bessie's revengeful spirit appears to taunt him: ". . . got those twelve one-thousand dollar bills ready? Or did you pass them out last night?"

The "darky," unaware of the presence of the ghost, appears to tell Abe: "Everything is alright, I'se got de carriage ready and dat train say it wait for you."

In the next scene, the trial begins with the appearance of the judge. The entire audience is required to rise when he enters, and it is thereafter caught up in being part of the drama. The play is popular and the auditorium is as packed as the courtroom was.

The first prosecution witness is Jennie, a "colored maid," who testifies that Bessie was very sad during the brief stay at the hotel. She cried a lot, and during the last night Abe struck her. In Jennie's words, "T'was most day 'fore she ebber quiet down." But the next morning she found Bessie to be "so smiley and nice" because she and her husband had "new plans." She saw them off to a midwinter picnic, with Bessie wearing all her diamonds. Consequently, the maid also testifies, "He had two of de lady's rings on him when he come back without her." The body had on the same clothes, she says, when she saw it in the funeral parlor, where, coincidentally, she worked at night. Her reaction to the clothing of the dead woman is one of exaggerated fright, with rolling of eyes and chattering of teeth.

The second prosecution witness is Morelli, a bartender at the Rose Bud Saloon, who also saw the couple before they left.[9] He testifies that he saw them on the fatal day and remembers them clearly: "The lady, she drank only a little wine, but he drank straight whiskey—damn good whiskey, too . . . the same as the judge here drinks." (His gesture to the bench amuses the audience). He further testifies that Abe came in the evening of the murder after sundown. "He was terrible nervous and just took one drink after another . . . . He was wearing two of them big diamond rings, the lady, she used to wear."

To return to history for a moment. In Jefferson there is a photograph and a painting of Abe and Bessie. He appears short and stocky, with blunt fingers; she was small and delicate. Even if he had been so indiscreet, or so inclined, to wear these lady's rings, he could not have gotten them on his fingers. As a consequence, doubt enters the mind of today's investigator, as it obviously did the jury of Abe's third trial.[10]

The first defense witness is a white "lady," Miss Belle Gouldy, who works at the funeral home in the daytime and has a much livelier and more profitable profession at night. She testifies that she had helped lay out the body of Bessie and that she had seen Bessie and Abe cross the bridge on the day of the picnic. Then she lays a bombshell.

"Then I seen her again on the next Thursday about 5:00 in the evening. I seen this Bessie Moore going across that bridge with a *strange* man. And if I say he's strange, *he is strange* . . . cause I get around more'n most *folks*."

She testifies that she saw Bessie on Thursday tightening her garter while crossing the bridge, two hundred yards away. Then, lo and behold, when she helped lay out the body, she saw that same garter—pinned over to make it tighter. A demonstration here on her own shapely leg impresses the all-male jury.

The second defense witness is the Justice of the Peace and Coroner for Marion County. His testimony is also significant. He testifies that the body could not have lain in the woods well preserved for two weeks. He mentions the strange fact that even the scraps of the picnic lunch had not been disturbed by animals. He refutes a doctor who said at the former trial that Bessie might have lain in a snow bank: "Snow melts rapidly in these parts. By the time the body was found, there had been days of 71 degrees temperature."

After amazingly good impromptu speeches by the defense and "the persecuting attorney," all twelve jurors vote for acquittal. Abe then rushes out to the train, in accordance with folk tradition.[11]

Historians would probably "check the record" by considering the written account in any source. Consider the following two.

In the *Texas Bar Journal*[12] I find this information about the beautiful and innocent Bessie, whose murder was described by the then Governor of Texas as "a crime unparalleled in the record of blood." The *Journal* is quoting a newspaper article on the beginning of the trial in 1878.

[The] history of Bessie's life is a sad story of sin, sorrow, and bloody tragedy. The facts are these: She was born in the City of Syracuse, New York, her maiden name being Annie Stone. She was the eldest daughter of a shoe dealer, a man with good business and in easy circumstances. Annie was given a liberal education and early manifested literary taste. Her great beauty and attractive manners drew around her many admirers and exposed her to temptations which resulted in her ruin. At the early age of fifteen she was seduced by a young man in Syracuse and is supposed to have been his mistress for some time. Afterwards she became a public prostitute and went to Cincinnati, where she became quite well known. During her stay there she was an inmate of an establishment kept by Miss Frank Wright. Her numerous diamonds received from her many admirers gave her the nick name of "Diamond Bessie."

She first met Rothschild at Hot Springs about 15 months before the fatal event. Rothschild soon gained a strange ascendency over her, which was continued until her death, in spite of the most cruel treatment. It is on record in the Justice Court of Cincinnati that he frequently beat and abused her shamefully, that while the Republican Convention was in session at Cincinnati he demanded that she should give him $50.00 per day, and when she failed to do this, he fell upon her in a great rage and treated her so violently that he was put under arrest.

About a fortnight before the murder, the pair left Cincinnati and went to Danville, Indiana, where they were married. They came to Texas. . . .

At the time of her death, Bessie was 23 years of age and still very beautiful. But she had become somewhat addicted to the use of stimulants and at times drank very hard. She is believed to have been intoxicated when she was led away to the woods.[13]

If historians consider only the written accounts of the event, they must consider a second one also. Twenty years after the murder, the editor of a Texarkana newspaper wrote that he, too, saw Abe and Bessie on that fatal day, January 21, 1877.

The writer himself, returning from a ride, met them within a hundred yards of the bridge and noticed them only sufficiently to note that they were strangers, fashionably dressed, and that the woman was very beautiful.

The couple strolled leisurely along for half a mile on the other side of the bridge, then taking a by path plunged into the forest, climbed a hill, almost within stone's throw of the public thoroughfare, and within rifle shot of the city itself. They had their lunch and doubtless the man, who planned one of the most cowardly murders ever perpetrated, whispered words of love and loyalty into the ears of the poor woman, only too glad to receive them. Their lunch was spread on a large rock, it was almost an ideal spot, deep in the heart of the woodland, surrounded by the songs of birds and the musical ripple of the running water; in the shade of the giant oak and ironwood they whiled away the midday hours; seated on the moss grown rock, the woman cut the initials of her husband in the soft bark of a curly maple and with a fond woman's foolish heart treasured the false vows of her brutal lord in whose inhuman breast lurked a purpose so dark, so deadly that the fiends of hell must have shuddered at its import. While the foolish heart of the woman fluttered with hope and thrilled with fond desires, the hand of the master murderer of modern times pushes the rim of a deadly revolver within an inch of her white temple, where rippling masses of sunny hair fell in clustering curls, and without a tremor sent a bullet crashing through her brain. The sound of a shot rang out on the evening air, reverberated from the hillside and died away in distant woods. The birds stopped midway their gladsome song, a tiny serpent of smoke rose above the tree tops and drifted with the winds, a frightened squirrel darted into its den, the sluggish river flowed smoothly at the base of the hill, and a dead white face stared at the winter sky.

Is that history? Well, that is the version which appeared in Jefferson's centennial history, 1936, and it has been reprinted many times.

This seems to indicate that the folklore of a particular period or region is as significant and accurate as newspaper clippings. More so, perhaps, because a newspaper article represents the opinions of one single man—the writer—while a legend, tale, anecdote, or folk drama, if it enters oral tradition, expresses the feelings of a great number. Such is the case of the "Diamond Bessie Murder Trial."

It is evident that the play is not history, but is it a folk drama? Fundamentally, it is. In brief, folk drama is of two kinds. It is drama which is anonymous, having been set in motion by someone long ago but added to traditionally, or it is "plays using folk material."

An example of the latter is Paul Green's dramatic productions, which are produced in the summer in several states, including Texas at Palo Duro Canyon. These productions are concerned with folk subject matters—with the legends, superstitions, customs, environmental differences, and the vernacular of the common people.

The Jefferson play is concerned with all of these, but it is not the work of a polished playwright like Green. Neither is it anonymous, for the script was outlined many years ago by a Mrs. Lawton

Riley who subsequently moved away from Jefferson. Her characters were selected from the transcript of the trial, but her dialogue has never been fully recorded.

Local lawyers, who play the major roles of the defense and the prosecution, know the history and legend of the trial and they ad-lib throughout. They do maintain from year to year the anecdotes that please the crowd. Abe Rothschild and Diamond Bessie are stereotyped villain and heroine, as they are popularly remembered, not as they were reported in some newspapers and law journals. The Negroes, fearful of ghosts, provide the same kind of stereotyped humor as in the minstrel days. The jury, made up of the Jefferson Lions Club, delights the audience with personal interpretations of their roles. One fat man snores loudly; the local undertaker never changes expression throughout the entire trial—oblivious of the antics of the lawyers. Lechery and guilt are shown by the men on the jury and the judge when the town prostitute is put on the stand.

It is interesting to note that the morality plays of the 15th century were "folk" in origin, with comic elements added to the religious theme. I was told in Jefferson that Mrs. Riley, an Episcopalian minister's wife, meant to outline a morality play.[14] It certainly is not played that way now. The good guys—the sheriff and the judge—are shown to be first-class hypocrites, as is the prosecuting attorney. The bartender, the prostitute, the glib defense attorney are obviously the favorites of the crowd. In the hands of the community players, the comic elements and legends have taken over, as the play was added to, and changed, from year to year. The history involved is "in a state of wreck"—but is very interesting if you are studying folkways, as well as dates and events.[15]

NOTES

1.   This is discussed in *A History of Jefferson: 1836-1936*, a pamphlet of 60 pages compiled by Mrs. Arch McKay and Mrs. H. A. Spellings for the centennial celebration. No publisher is given and five subsequent editions are not dated or updated.

2.   Not the beautifully restored Excelsior House, but "The Brooks House," which was destroyed by fire recently. Informant: Mrs. Mildred Warren, Commerce, Texas, September 1, 1970.

3. Américo Paredes, address to the American Folklore Society and the Sociedad Folklorica de Mexico, Mexico City, December 28, 1959.

4. This stereotype has been promoted by writers. "Jewish people from Jefferson had the jail cell, in which Rothschild was confirmed, carpeted and fitted up as a parlor . . . and he enjoyed the best of food," according to Henry Yelvington, *Ghost Lore*, San Antonio: Naylor Company, 1936, p. 119. In more modern times, a case has been ordered retried in Lufkin, Texas, because the prosecuting attorney referred to a witness as "that Jew," according to *Texas Observer*, November 23, 1962, p. 3.

5. Emphasis added.

6. Informant: Mrs. W. S. Terry, Jefferson, Texas, May 9, 1967, who obtained the "rough draft" for me.

7. The donor was Edward McDonald.

8. The "gay red cloak" and "gay little hat" mentioned are not factually accurate. Actually, court records show that she wore a black velvet hat with trim, kid shoes, silk or lisle stockings with a blue flower design in front, a pair of garters, alike but one white and one blue, a chemise of linen, a plain white underskirt, a flannel petticoat, a black silk shirt, a grey skirt of "waterproof" material, a woolen basque and polanaise, a very heavy black cloak with lap-over braid for the buttons, called a walking cloak, a collar, a purple necktie, and a "nondescript," with reference to which the witness said, "I do not know what it is and can't name it."

9. This part has been excellently played since 1954 by Elbert Wise, now almost 90, who has a genuine Italian accent.

10. The most realistic picture of Abe, owned by V. H. Hackney of Marshall, shows him in jail in·Marshall with Jim Currie, a detective who shot and killed a member of Maurice Barrymore's acting company. He, too, was freed because the also-wounded Barrymore didn't have time to come back to Texas to testify. Abe was described at the time as a "suave, bugeyed little dude," according to Frank X. Tolbert, *Dallas Morning News*, August 20, 1967, p. 21.

11. Anecdotes about the annual drama are also repeated in true folk tradition. During one performance the prosecuting attorney said at the height of his argument, "This man should be sent to the electric chair." Then he added quickly, "If there was such a thing."

12. Mahlon L. Walters, "Who Done It to Whom: Rothschild in Retrospect," *Texas Bar Journal*, February, 1963, quoting the *Dallas Commercial* on the day of the trial in 1878 (pages not given). Attorney Walters is said to have been one of the outstanding actors in the annual drama.

13. Walters. Today the woods are still there—a beautiful slope down toward

the bayou. Jefferson teen-agers refer to it as "Bessie's Bottom." Later newspaper accounts were not so explicit. The *Dallas Morning News*, Sunday, January 8, 1933, Section IV, p. 1, stereotyped the alleged murderer as "the dark and tall Abe Rothschild," who was "the son of a well known wealthy Eastern family." The body the article said was discovered by "a group of little Negroes"—"pickaninnies" who were "scairt plum green." This account is relied on completely by Yelvington, pages 116-123, who gives "some negro boys" some frightened dialogue in dialect when the "white 'oman" is discovered in her "red coat" and hat "pulled jauntily over. . .a gaping bullet hole."

14. Informant: Mrs. Kay Butler, Jefferson, Texas, May 10, 1967.

15. This article was prepared with the help of a Faculty Research Grant at East Texas State University in 1967.

Julia Nott Waugh
On Los Pastores

By JOHN IGO

JULIA Nott
Waugh left only two books and a stack of papers which Frank
Wardlaw, Director of the University of Texas Press, in a letter dated
January 28, 1959, described as "a collection of random and somewhat disorganized notes." But it was widely known that she was
"at work" on a book at the time of her death, probably the reworking of her Castroville book of 1934. She went to Europe to
gather fresh material for it; she was also collecting materials for a
work on the *pastorela* called *Los Pastores*.

Exactly what we lost by her death we shall never know. We can
only guess and be saddened. Until and unless her executors release
those "random" papers there is little to be done directly. But the
voice is not totally stilled.

In the early 1950's I became interested in Castroville. And everywhere I turned, the name Julia Nott Waugh came up. Then I also
became interested in the *Los Pastores* performances given at San
Jose; I became an enthusiast. And again someone mentioned the
name. Then in 1955 her book *The Silver Cradle* was published by
The University of Texas Press. It contained a chapter on *Los Pastores,* entitled "Babe of Beauty."

15

Although I had met her sometime earlier, I re-met her at the autograph party for *The Silver Cradle* at Rosengren's Book Store in San Antonio. My enthusiasms coincided with hers. I had found someone who knew firsthand all about the things I wanted to know about; and she was, I think, pleased to find a young man of the 'uncaring' generation who so obviously cared for things she held dear. We became telephone friends—always talking about *Pastores* or Castroville, but mostly *Pastores.* She was interested in *Los Pastores* as a folk activity of people she knew and loved in San Antonio, but she also had a cultural historian's interest in its European beginnings. Since I was the fledgling and knew little, I thought I was interested in everything about it.

I knew that *Los Pastores* is a traditional Spanish-language nativity drama either created or creatively adapted by the Franciscans in Mexico, who produced versions of it wherever their missionary work carried them. The colorful and intriguing mixture of local folk elements (such as the anti-clerical hermit, the lazy man and the nagging wife, the quarreling devils) with orthodox theology and a whopping good conflict of good and evil was a heady brew for me. I knew that there were places in San Antonio where one could manage to see it; but I did not know then that there were about half a dozen troupes in San Antonio, each working from different scripts; perhaps half a dozen more in Bexar County and surrounding counties; and probably a dozen or two more in the great overlap area of Spanish/English following the border from Brownsville to El Paso. The scripts, or books, containing the texts are laboriously transcribed from memory by the owners (there may have been an Ur-text, but it is long lost; the *Pastores* tradition is oral). And errors and variations incident to oral transmission creep in. There are versions in Mexico and in all the border states; they have strong basic similarities but they vary widely in detail.

The story is fairly constant in text and performance (there are staging traditions, too, that are not to be found in the text)—Luzbel and his demons hear that Jesucristo has been born and decide to attack mankind while the enemy is a helpless infant; shepherds on the way to Bethlehem are met and tempted by the demons and are defended by Michael the Archangel, who defeats Luzbel again; and the shepherds arrive at the Manger to adore the Christ Child.

That is the basic version. But the Infernal Council is grand theatrics, with shrieking devils (who deliberately frighten the children in the audience) and glorious demonic dialogue (which will intrigue any adult who listens carefully); the shepherds sing all along their journey to Bethlehem, and that makes a good show; there is a lot of fencing between Michael and Luzbel, and a duel is always exciting; the hermit character adds both Mexican humor and topical/local detail ad lib; and over all there is the local coloring—Gila the Hebrew shepherdess prepares *tacos, enchiladas, y tamales* for the shepherds, etc.; and, finally, there is the fervent if sentimental religious aspect, an audience-participation activity, during which the audience follows the shepherds to the Manger to kiss the foot of the Christ Child doll.

Where this *pastorela* started in the New World is still a matter of conjecture, but it goes back hundreds of years. Juan B. Rael has listed and treated about eighty versions and variants, but when I began to talk to Julia Nott Waugh I did not know there was such a richness to be found. All I knew was that she had information that could not be duplicated, especially on local versions that I might see. I knew of the Granados-Tranchese version and had learned of the Gertrudes Alonzo version by chance; and I suspected the existence of others. She led me slowly into the knowledge of several others, never so much at one time that I might be overwhelmed and back off, but enough to whet my appetite. She was full of counsel as well as information, and imparted method along with anecdote.

I thought that seeing the Guadalupe Troupe (the Granados-Tranchese version) would be a good starting place, because it is performed between Christmas and New Year's at Mission San Jose; gently she informed me that each troupe performs it a number of times each year, never before Christmas Eve (it follows another work in the Franciscan Cycle, *Las Posadas*) and usually never later than Ash Wednesday, in churchyards and in the back yards of the performers—it is a great privilege to be host. It developed that there is no established place (other than the "public" performance at Mission San Jose) where one can count on seeing *Los Pastores*. The site shifts at the whim of the performers and the performance starts either later or earlier than announced, as it is convenient. One has to go looking, making telephone calls, inquiring of parish priests and filling station attendants.

But I did not know such things, then. They came piecemeal in my chats with Julia Nott Waugh.

Over the two years of our talks, she told me about various aspects of the same events or ideas. What I learned from her I have arranged in five divisions, none of which should be understood to report a conversation that took place all at one time. I cannot pretend that the accounts are verbatim, but they are as close as I could manage without dictation and shorthand. The intention of the sentences is hers and sometimes the full phrasing. The first interview was a casual chat on November 1, 1955, as I drove her home from Rosengren's.

ONE

Q: I wish I had seen one of the performances at the Chapel of Miracles.

A: Frequently in the early days, *Los Pastores* lasted from 9:00 till 2:00 or 3:00. A full-length *Pastores* would be intolerable to a modern audience, especially Anglo. But I never tired of it. I have seen them all, but the Alonzo-Uriega is the one I know best.

There is another *Pastores* troupe being organized. They have all the actors, and they have a director. They all know the lines and the business. It will be a completely new production, in competition with the one at the Mission [the Granados-Tranchese version at Mission San Jose]. There is only one thing wrong—all the actors and the director have been in other performances of *Los Pastores* in other places, and they are all willing, but they all know different texts. And they cannot reconcile what they have. It is a problem. [She gave no clue to identities or location.]

About a year later, having resorted to the out-of-print market, I asked permission to drop by her home to have her sign two copies of her *Castro-Ville and Henri Castro, Empresario* (San Antonio, 1934). That day we talked about Castroville and the last Castro diary.

On January 3, 1957, again in pursuit of *Pastores* information, I called her.

TWO

Q: I have never seen a *Pastores* except at the Mission. Are the others readily available? how do I see one? are they all pretty much alike?

A: There are at present three troupes of *Pastores* players. The Kenwood group, from Cementville. They have not been very active in recent years, but they are going strong this year. And good. Their Luzbel has been ill. Their book is different from the Granados one, with variations many will not notice. And they have cunning baby devils, but don't mind that—baby devils have been done for generations.

The Guadalupe group, using the Granados book. It is so illogical—Father Tranchese put it together and made it logical. That's all right. It's been being changed for centuries. He used songs not used hereabouts, which is fine—used them because he liked them. But they had to consult the Uriega MS. Mrs. Gutierrez [née Uriega] told me that they borrowed the copy belonging to her husband [Martin Gutierrez]. So you see, that one [Granados-Tranchese] is sort of a mixture of the two MSS.

See it at the Church, though [Guadalupe Church].

The Losoya group, based on the Uriega MS. It is seldom performed in public. It is usually done in yards—it is more colorful there. They haven't been active in years, or at least not much, but now it is being revived because of the poor quality of the Granados performance.

And there may even be a fourth troupe. I have heard of one, but not lately. After a little telephoning, I shall have more specific information about the fourth troupe. [The group she mentioned in November, 1955? She did not find out anything.]

Having learned in the interview that she did not have a copy of the Guadalupe Church *Las Posadas* published by Betancourt, I sent her one. That prompted a thank-you note on January 7, 1957, and another telephone interview the next day.

THREE

Q: In your book, it was the Alonzo version, wasn't it? That is the one I want to see.

A: The Uriega, the Francisco Uriega, family of Losoya, Texas, south of San Jose about ten miles, has a manuscript of *Los Pastores.* Francisco was the first shepherd—which is unusual because the director-leader is usually one of the devils. His sister married Martin Gutierrez, who is now first shepherd in the troupe. Mrs. Uriega Gutierrez is acting as prompter this year.

In the old Alonzo-Uriega troupe there were two groups: the shepherds, all Uriegas (all lean boys) and the devils, all Gutierrezes (all fat boys). The devils acted from the book of Gertrudes Alonzo [the Doroteo of her book] and the shepherds acted simultaneously from the Uriega Book, without conflict. Uriega had apparently, in recording the whole show from memory, remembered the shepherds' parts better—even though his manuscript is by far the longest of those in this area; Alonzo in recording his, apparently remembered the devils' parts better, although his too is longer than the Cementville MS.

Gertrudes Alonzo has retired because of age. And he has kept his manuscript. So the production this year—the first in years—is completely from the Uriega (now Gutierrez) Book. They always call a MS "the Book."

I took Alonzo to the performance at the house of Blas Rodriguez on Mayfield Boulevard last Sunday night [January 6, 1957]. He was greeted with great deference by all the older members of the cast, who remembered him as the most magnificent Luzbel within their experience—or mine.

The outstanding feature of this show is the completeness of the performance. It includes details that the others have never had and some they omit. That Guadalupe manuscript is the most butchered and fragmentary of all—it is patched and shuffled.

Both the Alonzo and the Uriega-Gutierrez MSS are in handwritten copies in ledgers. I gave them a new ledger to make a new copy—the old one is tattered [this is apparently the Alonzo MS she means]. And I had the Uriega-Gutierrez MS typed for them as a gift, sometime back, so that they have a typed copy now to work from.

Alonzo is a remarkable man. He could hardly read and was worse at writing. So he hired, poor as he was, a man to write from dictation the manuscript he has. It survived as a good manuscript even though he could not have added to it himself.

Q: It is good to know about second copies. Something might happen to the only copy, and it would be lost forever.

A: Oh, I am not worried about the loss of the MSS. The families treasure them even when they don't appreciate fully what they have.

Again on February 2, 1957, in a telephone conversation, she chatted about *Los Pastores*. I think she was happy to have me so avid about details. When I did not press for name, date, place, she would ask if I wanted to know; I always did, and she always supplied them.

FOUR

Q: I saw both the Cementville and the Losoya troupes last month and took extensive notes.

A: Well, go again. You have to be familiar enough to sort out the accidental things in a performance from the standard. And you need to compare them by going back and forth between them.

The Gutierrez players are performing tonight [it was at the home of Blas Rodriguez again, according to Simon Gutierrez, in a letter dated January 27, 1957]. Their version, though crippled by the illness of the players from time to time, is the most conscientious about following the script. It has been about eight years since their last season of performing; they are a little shaky this year. But next year, they will be back at their best.

The Guadalupe players will give two more performances: one

on Saturday, February 9, at a Negro church on Nolan; the other on Sunday, February 10, at the Immaculate Heart of Mary, on South Concho Street.

The last interview, October 2, 1957, was far more formal. I visited her at her home, armed with what she called my 'intimidating' notebook and a set of questions. She took me on a tour of the house, showed me her 'bite-sized' bedroom balcony, let me handle her treasured mementos. Finally we settled, and she chatted about things, veering in an easy swoop from what she had been saying to what the next question triggered in that fertile memory and imagination. She paused sometimes, thinking; but I suspect that sometimes she paused to let me get down some detail she liked. It was a coffee-cup chat. Several times the storyteller in her took over and I abandoned the questions.

FIVE

Q: Do you speak Spanish? read it?

A: Not fluent Spanish—enough to communicate, without benefit of syntax. I can handle verbs and nouns, and I let the rest have their way.

Q: Why the book, *The Silver Cradle*?

A: An interest in the ceremonies led me to it. I got to know the people—that led to an interest in the things they do. I have an affinity for Latins—and a capacity for returning again and again [for *Los Pastores*] and liking it.

Q: Do a whole book on *Los Pastores*. Expand the chapter and go from there.

A: I nearly did a book on it. The *Pastores* chapter in the *Cradle* was much longer. It was cut severely—edited down to its present size. Now you want it back as it was.

Q: Was the book fiction originally? I've heard it was.

A: No. It started from a very high level, third-person essay—and went to personality. The original introductory essay is now the first chapter. I tried to capture colors, rhythms, and essences, rather than carefully ordered essay treatment of socio-economics, etc.

Q: Is the book based on real people?

A: The school teacher, his sister, Doroteo, Parrado, and the owner of the cradle are real people, real individuals. Doroteo was Gertrudes Alonzo; Parrado was Francisco Uriega. [The book was dedicated to Alonzo and Uriega.] Some are composites. There are no fictional people or events, if that's what you mean.

Q: How did you gather material? where? how long?

A: From miscellaneous writing I did: features, articles in various publications—the Catholic press, but don't look. I will revise the good and omit the weak. I spent twenty-five years in gathering materials, doing articles, all unrelated; I found much misinformation and even repeated some of it. I decided to arrange the articles as a series. It grew steadily from there.
And Mrs. Gutierrez helped.
I gathered my best material firsthand, too. One night, Luzbel's vegetable truck with devils and the hermit dropped me at the corner of Concho and Buena Vista. It was too late for a bus, so I waited for a taxi among the drunks and floozies. A man stopped and offered me a ride. I preferred human companionship there without a phone to highway robbers, so I declined. The man I had declined to ride with sent a taxi to pick me up.
I went to the *Posadas* in homes. Strangers are not intruders if they care, you know. One night I saw a candle in a window and a line of people. It was as cold as Christian charity. I went in. Nothing happened. Hours passed. I sat in a corner. People drifted in and out. But I waited. There was subdued excitement. Then came the *levantada* [the taking up of the infant Jesus from the manger on

Candlemas, the conclusion of the Christmas enactments]. That was, perhaps, the real genesis of the book.

Q: Is there a silver cradle?

A: Yes, there is. Small, pure silver.
I want to tell you a story before I forget.
Gertrudes Alonzo, for years the dean of Luzbels in this region, lived in an unclean neighborhood in a filthy shack. He was condemned by the Board of Health. His shack was demolished and the area was cleaned up. He of course had to live elsewhere. But he had to keep moving. Nobody would put up with his troupe's singing *Los Pastores* from dark till past midnight several nights a week. They'd complain. He'd be put out. A local undertaker had a huge auditorium upstairs over the chapel and workrooms—heaven only knows why—where its presence was unsuspected—a huge auditorium dominated by two pictures, a cheap Our Lady of Guadalupe and a huge picture of FDR. On a bench in a back corner a tired ancient crone was allowed to sleep. The ceiling was low, which made for much reverberation. And noises of all sorts floated up from the workrooms below. And there for one whole autumn, three nights a week, about fifteen strong-voiced Mexicans roared through the entire play, punctuated but not interrupted by thumping coffins, screeching tires, banging doors, clattering cans. The din was magnificent and awesome, but nobody downstairs could hear it. Even if they had heard it, nobody would have believed it—who would admit he could hear a choir of bellowing male voices, singing *Pastores* music, coming down from the ceiling of a funeral home that had, so far as anyone knew, no second floor?

Q: Have you done anything other than the two published books? anything unpublished or in the works?

A: The articles I mentioned. Right now I am reading on the *pastorela* in French and Spanish, everything available. I have another book in the process. [She was working, or reworking, the book on Castroville.] And another two in mind. [Q: Fiction?] A: Oh, no, no fiction!

The trip to Europe this fall is important—with perhaps some side trips to look for more on *Pastores.*

We chatted at least a couple of hours, but I came home with several of my original questions untouched, and a packet of notes on things I had not had the wisdom to ask. I held the notebook, she conducted that interview. She was recording things. I left, promising to return. I never saw her again.

The next communication I had from her was a card from Nice, France, postmarked January 6, 1958, with a view of the Spanish Steps in Rome. The message: "Keats died in the house on the right. . . .Home in about three weeks, knowing little more about *Los Pastores* than when I left. Julia N. Waugh."

She died, on the way home, in the Algonquin Hotel, Manhattan, on January 18, 1958.

NOTES

Los Pastores: MSS, troupes, and locations mentioned directly or by inference in the interviews and narration above.

Gertrudes Alonzo MS: Guadalupe Church, San Antonio

Leandro Granados (Granados-Tranchese) MS: Guadalupe Church

Mariano Rodriguez MS: San Antonio College

Prospero Baca MS: García Collection, University of Texas

Luzbel en Campaña: San Diego, Texas parish church

Uriega-Gutierrez MS: Martin Gutierrez, San Antonio

The Dolorosa Street version MS: displaced by Urban Renewal

The Pastores Street version MS: accidentally destroyed

Kenwood (Cementville) MS: St. Anthony Shrine (Ramon Patino MS)

Candelaria Rodriguez MS: reported at Christ the King Church

Sarah Smith King MS: (from Chapel of Miracles?) reported to be with her heirs in California

Approximately 20 different MS versions are in the Heinrich Collection, Our Lady of the Lake College

Approximately 20 different versions are available at the San Antonio College Library

Semana Santa In Seville

By CHARLES B. MARTIN

SEVILLE, located in the heart of Andalucia, is noted both for its many historical and architectural treasures and for its religious and secular festivals. The chief architectural landmark is the Giralda tower, a Moorish minaret, which stands next to the third largest church in Christendom and the largest Gothic cathedral in Europe. A nearby attraction is the Alcazar Palace, also a legacy of the Moors. Along the Alcazar wall lies the ancient Barrio de Santa Cruz, once the old Jewish quarter, a section with narrow cobblestone streets, flower-filled balconies, tiny plazas filled with roses and orange trees. The old tobacco factory of *Carmen*, surrounded by a moat, has been remodeled to become the University of Seville, next door to the Andalucia Palace, the luxury hotel.

The most typical fiestas in Seville are Semana Santa (Holy Week) and the Feria de Abril (April Fair), both of which have become famous, attracting dignitaries from all over the world, not to mention a *romería* (or pilgrimage) at Whitsuntide from Seville and nearby villages to Rocio, where according to legend, the Virgin appeared to a shepherd.

While the April Fair is decidedly secular in nature—with hundreds of tiny *casetas* (or canvas houses), horse parades every day, bullfights every afternoon—Holy Week is a much more somber affair, the product of four hundred years of public religious devotion during Passiontide.

Holy Week consists of seven days of processions. A procession is made up of a band playing funeral marches, a large group of penitents, and one or two floats (called *pasos*), carried by men underneath. Each procession begins at a given hour of the day from a particular church, passes along a predetermined route to the cathedral, and from there returns home via the shortest route. Since the procession stops every two or three thousand yards to allow the men some rest, the entire journey can vary from three and a half hours, the shortest time, to eleven hours, the longest, depending, of course, on the distance between the parish church and the cathedral. There are fifty-two religious brotherhoods (or *cofradías*) in Seville; hence there are approximately seven processions a day, with the exception of Good Friday, which has thirteen—six in the early morning and seven in the late afternoon. The last of these doesn't reach its home church until 2:30 Saturday morning. Then on Saturday afternoon, there are only three processions, one beginning at 3:15 p. m. and the last at 5:30. Thus the visitor can go out at about any hour of the day or night and see a procession winding its way to or from the cathedral.

Holy Week festivities actually begin on Palm Sunday when the first *paso* (or float) emerges from the suburban San Sebastian Church at 2:45 in the afternoon for a ten-hour journey to the cathedral and back. It is particularly impressive as it moves through the shady María Louisa park preceded by a military band, the *cruz de guía* (or guiding cross), the *nazarenos* (nazarenes, i. e. Holy Week "pilgrims") in pointed hoods and sandals, interspersed with persons carrying banners and insignia of both the church and the confraternity.

The members who follow the float are *penitentes*; they walk barefoot and carry wooden crosses. They are the true penitents of Holy Week and are fulfilling a promise to do penance in return for some answered prayer, which was earlier recorded in the book of brotherhood. Their hats are not pointed but rather are folded down their backs. Some have been seen to wear chains on their feet, though I myself saw none this past year.

28 : CHARLES B. MARTIN

The tunic-like gowns of the *nazarenos* can be made of simple cloth or expensive silk and can be belted with either a wide sash or a rope. The insignia of the *cofradía* usually appears on the front of the hoods.

If the *cofradía* has a second *paso*—and most of them do—it contains an image of the Virgin, called by various names—Our Lady of Grace and Hope, Our Lady of the Star, Holy Mary of the Waters, and so on. Her *paso* is always covered with a gold-embroidered canopy supported by twelve hand-carved silver rods, which sway while the *paso* is in motion and thus add a graceful sparkle to the fringed canopy. The Virgin wears a gold or silver crown and a long robe, also elaborately embroidered with gold or silver on silk, which extends ten to fifteen feet from her shoulders to the back of the *paso*. Her bosom is often decked with jewels and she stands amid hundreds of silver candelabra and silver-embossed vases filled with white carnations. The most famous Virgin is La Marcarena, whose breast blazes with emeralds and who has real diamonds for tears.

Although the *pasos* may weigh as much as 10,000 pounds each, they are still carried by thirty to seventy paid men rather than motor-driven vehicles, as is done in Malaga. Originally the floats had simple stems both fore and aft and could be carried by a small number of men. However, as they increased in size, it became necessary for more men to help bear the weight and for legs to be added to support the *paso* while the men rest.

Those who carry the *pasos* are called *costaleros,* from *costal,* the cushion-like head gear which protects their heads and necks. No such thing as a yoke exists under the float to rest on the *costaleros'* shoulders. Rather, a series of grooves are cut in the 2 x 4's under the platform, and the men are lined up and assigned positions according to size, with the tallest men in the front row and the shortest behind.

A leader next to the float calls out instructions and taps a metal knocker on the front of the float as a signal for the men to raise it up in unison. Then they all march in step to a drum and bugle corps.

For such arduous work each *costalero* is paid approximately $8.00 to $10.00 for a job which may take ten or more hours. Many of these men will work for another *cofradía* or two during the week, according to the durability of their feet and shoulders.

The *penitentes* and *nazarenos*, as official members of the organization, receive no pay. Those who are unmasked and carry banners, altar candles, or the heavy silver trumpets do receive from $2.00 to $3.00 for their work. A great deal of money is spent on candles, flowers, and bands; each *cofradía* spends from $2,000 to $4,000 on one Holy Week procession. Traditionally this expense has been met by the local brotherhood, but in recent years the City Hall has had to lend its support. Rumor has it that the national government in Madrid, presumably the Department of Tourism, offered financial aid last year so that the show might go on—for reasons economic rather than religious.

Unless one understands something of the nature of this ancient religious festival, he might easily become bored with what seems endless repetition of the same thing. To absorb the atmosphere of Holy Week fully, he must seek out those certain places where the local practices display the religious fervor of a particular parish.

Such moments occur when a *paso* leaves its home church. After it emerges from the church door, someone bursts into a spontaneous, wailing, prayerful song, called a *saeta*. In its improvised verses, it tells of Christ's anguish, who suffered to redeem mankind, or of the solitude and sorrow of the Virgin Mary, who witnessed the humiliation of her son. *Saetas* sung to the Virgin are illustrated in this sorrowful one to La Macarena, the most venerated Mary of all Seville:

> Why do you cry, Mother mine,
> So beautiful and sorrowful,
> Since there is no one in the Macarena
> Who would not offer his life
> To remove your pain?
> Dove who from the heavens
> Made in Sevilla her nest,
> Stop for a moment your flight
> And in your favorite neighborhood
> Give happiness and consolation.

It is most impressive at night to see a long line of *penitentes* winding their way through the narrow streets and the flickering of hundreds of candles on the floats as they jerk along to the rhythmic steps of the *costaleros*.

Just getting a *paso* out the front door of a church can create a problem. One church had a Gothic archway so low that the *costaleros* had to get on their knees and sway back and forth so that each silver rod holding the canopy could clear the arched doorway.

Each *paso* arrives at a given point downtown, Plaza de la Campana, to begin the *carrera oficial,* or official route, and continues up Sierpes Street to the City Hall, where the brotherhood asks permission to continue to the cathedral. The procession enters the front of the cathedral, stops briefly before the Holy Sacrament, and leaves the cathedral by the back door to return to its respective church by the shortest possible way. Upon arrival home, more *saetas* are sung and there is general rejoicing on the part of the local parish.

On Holy Thursday many Spanish girls dress in black with lace mantillas and visit seven churches (representing the seven stations of the cross) for a brief period of devotion.

Good Friday is the busiest day for processions and actually might be considered two days in one, since six processions begin between 1:00 and 3:00 and seven more follow in the late afternoon. The two most popular of these dawn processions are *Nuestra Señora de la Esperanza,* more familiarly called La Macarena, and *Jesús de Gran Poder* (Jesus the Mighty). More than a thousand penitents accompany Jesus the Mighty, a 17th-century work by Juan de Mesa, one of the most venerated pieces of sculpture in the city. A special guard dressed like Roman soldiers with plumed helmets accompanies La Macarena; they are almost too theatrical and commercial for a religious procession. In fact, this brotherhood was mildly censured for its gaudy and theatrical pomp.

Only three *pasos* are carried through the streets on Saturday afternoon. The last one is traditionally Our Lady of Loneliness, with the sole figure of Mary grieving before an empty black cross over which a linen sash has been draped, for the removal of the dead Savior.

Thus the week ends on a rather somber and sorrowful note as the last *paso* with its empty cross moves slowly to its home parish. One experiences a sense of sorrow and relief as well as a sense of utter fatigue, particularly if he has kept up with most of the processions during the week. One also expects Easter Sunday to be some kind of grand climax to this vigorous week of penitential devotion. But when my wife and I were there, Easter Sunday was an anticlimax, with peaceful and quiet, deserted streets, though presumably some worshipers had gone to early mass. The cathedral on that day had its usual sprinkling of Sunday visitors, but most signs of Holy Week were gone except for a thin layer of wax on the cathedral floor and surrounding streets from the drippings of so many thousands of candles carried by thousands of faithful Nazarenes and penitents in their yearly devotion.

For the bystander the week may seem too commercial, too much a spectacle for tourists, something more profane than sacred, yet who can question someone else's devotion or someone else's motives? Yet even if one's thoughts and feelings may indeed at times become skeptical, there is still something very haunting in the muffled drums and the shrill trumpets of the funeral marches of *Semana Santa*.

The Decoration Of Graves
In Central Texas
With Seashells

By SARA CLARK

ASK anyone
what is the most common decoration found on graves in central
Texas and he'll say flowers, of course—real flowers and, now, plastic flowers. Ask him why flowers and he'll probably say because
they're pretty. Ask him if there's any other reason and he might
say because flowers are bright and drive away the loneliness and
coldness from a grave. He might go a step further and say that the
life of a flower is as fragile as a human life and its beauty as transient and that for this reason flowers are appropriate decorations for
graves. He might even say that the flowers on a grave are a symbol
for earthly life and an emblem of its short-lived pleasures.

But if you ask the ordinary central Texan what is the second
most common type of grave decoration found in this area, he probably won't be able to answer you—and he will likely be very surprised when you tell him that it is sea shells, a much more durable,
much less transient decoration than flowers, even the plastic varieties.

The shell-decorated graves in Central Texas can be divided into
four types. Type I consists of loose shells, most often freshwater
clams and mussels, arranged in a border or scattered over the sur-

33

face of the grave, which has been scraped clean of grass. This kind of grave is found more often in rural cemeteries than in urban ones. The Phillips cemetery, two miles south of Dripping Springs, contains some fine examples of this type of grave decoration.

In a second type of grave decoration using shells, a single large marine shell, usually a huge queen conch or whelk, ten inches or more in length, is placed on the grave or on the head- or foot-stone. Type II graves are found commonly in both urban and rural cemeteries. There are at least five graves with Type II decorations in the Oakwood cemetery in Austin.

These first two types involve loose shells laid on the grave or gravestone. In the third and fourth types the shells are embedded in cement and thus permanently fixed to the gravesite.

In Type III the grave is covered with a mound of concrete in which shells, most often giant Atlantic cockles, have been embedded, their concave sides down. Other shells are sometimes used. There is one grave of this sort in Blanco, Texas, made with huge queen conch shells embedded with their apertures facing outward; and there are several in Comfort and New Braunfels which use other bivalves besides cockles. Usually the shells are arranged over the entire mound of concrete, often in geometric patterns. Graves of this sort were made by both professional and amateur cement finishers. Most of the professionally made ones in this area are in the communities centering around New Braunfels and settled by German immigrants. The Comal cemetery in that city has many fine Type III graves.

The fourth type of shell decoration is found almost exclusively on the graves of Mexican-Americans. The grave is usually marked by a handmade concrete cross or other headstone and is bordered by a concrete curbing. Into the concrete of both the cross and the curbing have been set many kinds of decorative items: marbles, costume jewelry, broken crockery, colored tiles, and seashells. The color and originality of these Type IV grave decorations is striking. I have seen them in the cemeteries and *panteóns* of Austin, New Braunfels, Houston, and Brownsville, and of Matamoros across the river in Mexico.

In the Dripping Springs community in Hays County, I spoke with two elderly gentlemen who were descendants of people buried in the Phillips cemetery in graves with Type I shell decorations, the loose river shells. Frank Sansom, who was born in Dripping Springs in 1884, recalls that his family brought the shells back in tow sacks after fishing trips to the Pedernales when he was a child, but whether the shells were brought back for the purpose of putting them on graves is unclear. His parents, who died in 1916 and 1918, are buried in shell-covered graves.

Harvey King is a survivor of another family buried in graves of this type. He recalls that the shells his family used came from the San Marcos River near Fentress. His mother made borders for the flower beds in the front yard out of them. When a daughter, Ethel, died at the age of thirteen in 1910, the mother made a border of the shells around her grave. Seven years later when the mother died, the father and son put shells on her grave too, and after the father's death the son, Harvey King, carried on the family's tradition. Today the shells no longer form borders but are grouped loosely over the head portion of each grave.

Two striking grave decorations in the Phillips cemetery were constructed by Ray Kelley of Dripping Springs for the graves of his daughter Violet, who died in 1948 at the age of seventeen, and his wife Emma, who died in 1960. These graves are of Type III, a concrete mound in which shells have been embedded, mostly giant Atlantic cockles and small sea clams. He built hard covers over the graves so that the earth would not crack as the graves settled; he put shells on them because they were pretty. First he made a low form of one-inch mesh chicken-wire and poured concrete over it. He then stuck the shells, which he had gathered from Baytown on Galveston Bay and from Padre Island near Corpus Christi, into the wet cement. The larger cockleshells he placed in a line down the center of the graves and around the edges of his wife's grave and then he filled in the other areas with the smaller shells. A vestige of the originally brilliant colors of the shells remains on Mrs. Kelley's grave, although long exposure to the sun has bleached most of them.

In the Comal cemetery in New Braunfels there are many professionally made graves of Type III. The shells are giant Atlantic cockleshells arranged in orderly rows, and the cement work is usually marked with a large oval shape made in the cement when it was

Type I.

Type II.

wet. The mark includes these words: "Made by H. T. Mordhorst, New Braunfels, Tex."

Henry Theodore Mordhorst was a cement finisher who lived in New Braunfels from 1900 until his death in 1928. He was born in 1864 in Rostock, Germany, and came to the United States in 1882 with his mother and three sisters after the death of his father. The family settled first in Pomeroy, Ohio, and came to New Braunfels in 1900. In partnership with another man Mordhorst first made cement blocks for building; he later went into business for himself, making cement sidewalks, cellars, fireplaces, cisterns, wells, tombstones, curbings, monuments, dipping vats for cattle, and the shell-decorated grave covers.

In making his grave covers, Mordhorst first made a flat concrete base on which a wooden form was placed to mold the concrete. He used wire mesh, just as Ray Kelley did in Dripping Springs, to give the concrete support internally when it was poured into the mold. The shells were filled with cement and a wire was twisted into each one to help hold the shell to the grave cover. He arrived at this method of attaching the shells by experimentation after his earlier shells came off too easily.

He ordered the cockleshells from Rockport and Galveston; they arrived by train in big barrels. His daughter, Mrs. Val Schriewer of Seguin, related an anecdote about his shell orders. In 1918, during the war, he suddenly stopped receiving his shipments of shells. Letter after letter to the coast brought no reply. Finally a letter came from Washington advising him that he had been thoroughly investigated and cleared of any suspicion of subversive activities. The government had intercepted these orders for "shells," on the supposition that these German immigrants were ordering ammunition from the coast. The government officials must have been surprised and embarrassed to learn that the "shells" were simply seashells. From then on Mordhorst's orders went through with no trouble.

Mordhorst made these graves in towns all around the area: Blanco, Comfort, Boerne, Seguin, Kyle, Lockhart, Uhland, Sisterdale, Smithson Valley, Spring Branch, Fischer's Store, Sattler, Geronimo, and many others.

There are very few surviving relatives of persons whose graves have Mordhorst's shell-decorated covers who remember much about the process of construction. Most of the people who had direct dealings with Mordhorst are now dead.

Miss Hilda Linnartz, whose grandfather Balthaser Preiss established a family plot which contains six magnificent shell-decorated graves, recalls that people wanted the graves covered with concrete to prevent them from sinking and cracking open. She dislikes the shell decorations because when the shells are broken by hail or freezing, it is very difficult to get them replaced. She recalls that her mother had to have some broken shells replaced on the graves of her parents.

Mrs. Erno Neuse, two of whose grandparents, August and Dorothea Kirchner, died in 1917 and 1916 respectively and are buried under grave covers made by Mordhorst, also dislikes the broken shells and the fact that Mordhorst used too much gravel in his concrete so that some of the grave covers and curbings have broken. Since his customers paid high prices for his work and permanence was an object, they resent what they feel was inferior workmanship.

The past sexton of the Comal cemetery, Mr. George Linnartz, agreed that this use of shells as decorations was discontinued because after hail or frost broke the shells an ugly lump of cement was exposed which no other shell would fit. There are some graves in Blanco from which all the shells have been removed, so that very peculiar looking mounds of cement covered with lumps remain.

No one knows where Henry Mordhorst first got the idea for the beautiful shell-decorated grave covers that he made. They do not seem to be modeled closely after anything he knew in Germany. His two daughters, Mrs. Herbert Waldschmidt of San Antonio and Mrs. Val Schriewer of Seguin, believe that the idea was his own creation and his alone. "There was no one ever even to try and copy one," according to Mrs. Schriewer. The fact that many of the graves which bear these shell-decorated covers are dated before his arrival in New Braunfels in 1900 is given two plausible explanations by his daughters. Mrs. Waldschmidt said, "Now about those graves— well, my daddy made them but the graves were there before and then he put the shells on and the date they passed away." Mrs. Schriewer offered this explanation: "The reason for the graves dating back to 1880 or 1890 was some of the bodies were moved from

Type III.

Type IV.

the surrounding territory and moved to different places, which Daddy did alone. Sometimes he had as many as five and six bodies to take from one cemetery to another."

It is my feeling that Henry Mordhorst's Type III graves are some of the few professionally made examples of an art which is a tradition. Ray Kelley of Dripping Springs, who had never heard of Mordhorst or seen his graves, made two very similar ones by hand, and I am told that amateur versions like Kelly's are found all over the southern United States. In the Oakwood cemetery in Austin are two graves of this type which date from the 1860's. These are the graves of a Confederate official and his wife and the covers were most likely made by someone other than Mordhorst. That the art didn't die with Henry Mordhorst is shown by the presence of several graves in the Comal cemetery which are dated after 1928. One lady in New Braunfels recalls having a shell-covered grave made for her mother in the Mordhorst manner in 1937, nine years after the old man's death.

Mordhorst, Kelley, Sansom, and King are all participants in a well-established and widespread custom throughout the southern United States of decorating graves with seashells. There are shell-decorated graves on the Alabama-Coushatta Reservation and in Negro cemeteries in East Texas. In rural north Louisiana shells are often used to form borders for graves.[1] A number of years ago a grave was found in the Denton, Texas, burial ground[2] that was decorated with a shell of cast iron. One widely traveled and observant cemetery-hound from Georgia reports the use of shells in grave decoration "from Texas to Virginia and from Louisiana to Missouri."[3]

Whether this tradition is practiced all over the United States or not, I do not know. There is some indication that it may be a tradition brought from Europe. Several European folklorists have reported that shells have been used to decorate graves within the last century in Sweden, northern Germany, and in Dalmatia.[4] A French movie shows the custom in rural France in the early 1940's.[5]

In many prehistoric European settlements shells were buried with the bodies. In one paleolithic French grave the shells were arranged symmetrically on the skeleton, by pairs: four on the forehead, one on each hand, two on each foot, four on the knees and ankles.[6] Elsewhere a male skeleton wearing ornaments and a crown of perforated shells was found near a female skeleton which had been literally covered with shells, somewhat in the manner, I gather, of the graves in the Dripping Springs cemetery. Many of these shells had been transported great distances from the places where they occurred naturally. The religious historian E. O. James has stated that the shells commonly found in European paleolithic graves were for "magico-religious purposes connected with the restoration of life to the deceased."[7] He suggests that this ancient use of shells in connection with death in Europe is associated with the worship of an Indo-European fertility goddess whose cult spread across all of Europe and the western part of Asia. Among the many later embodiments of this goddess were the Sumerian Inanna, the Babylonian Ishtar, the Egyptian Isis, and the Greek Aphrodite, a goddess who was closely associated with shells.

Aphrodite's shell became an important motif on the burial urns of the ancient Greeks around 400 B. C.[8] She is depicted emerging from the scallop shell, the shell most common in her cult. She was said to have been born of a shell in the sea, and offerings of scallop shells were made at her shrines.

During the period of the Roman Empire the shell-motif was used on elaborate funerary monuments. Often a carved scallop shell formed a half-dome over a nich in which stood a portrait bust of the deceased or under which opened the tomb itself.[9] This architectural motif of the shell over the niche was destined to become an important embellishment centuries later in Renaissance and Baroque architecture.[10] Sometimes a carved shell crowned the Roman gravestone; in the late empire it provided the decorative motif for marble sarcophagi. Frequently Roman lead coffins were decorated with shell motifs, and one Roman lead coffin found in France contained five actual scallop shells.[11] Throughout the Empire shells and shell-motifs were connected with Roman burial.

The religious historian Mircea Eliade has written that people of many cultures have associated shells with their funerary customs.[12] He writes that the shell symbolizes eternal life because of its watery origin and because of the superficial resemblance of some shells to the female sexual organs. A shell can be used to symbolize birth and hence rebirth and hence eternal life.

We seem to have come a long way from Dripping Springs and New Braunfels. Would I tell that incredulous central Texan that the Kelleys and the Sansoms and the Kings of Dripping Springs used shells to decorate their graves because shells are a symbol for water, the great purifier and restorer? Would I suggest that H. T. Mordhorst promised eternal life to his customers and guaranteed it with cockleshells? Not exactly. Mr. King and Mr. Kelley and Mr. Sansom say that the shells were put on the graves because they are pretty and because "Mama did it." A New Braunfels monument dealer denies that the shells on Mordhorst's graves serve any function other than a decorative one, and the survivors of the old cement finisher's customers say they know of no significance to the shells, no good luck associated with their use.

So I wouldn't say that graves are decorated with shells in central Texas because of any powers attributed to the shells by their users. I would say that here in twentieth-century Texas exists a probable remnant of an ancient and widespread association of sea shells with human burial. King and Kelley and Sansom and Mordhorst were all participants in a tradition that is older and more significant than they were aware of and that may indeed have continued quietly but steadily since prehistoric times in Europe. The custom has lost its symbolic meaning and magical power but has survived simply because it is traditional and because it has decorative value.

NOTES

1. Fred Kniffen, "Necrogeography in the United States," *Geographical Review*, LVII (1967), pp. 426-427.

2. Dorothy Jean Michael, "Grave Decoration," *Backwoods to Border*, Publications of the Texas Folklore Society, XVIII (Dallas, 1943), 129-136.

3. Mr. Donald J. Jeane, Department of Geography, University of Georgia, Athens, Georgia, personal letter dated February 6, 1969.

4. Personal letters from the following persons:

   Professor Carl-Hermann Tillhagen, Nordiska Museet, Folkminnessamlingen, Stockholm, Sweden, September 17, 1969.

   Professor Walter Havernick, Director, Seminar fur Deutsche Altertums-

und Volkskunde, Museum für Hamburgische Geschichte, Hamburg, Germany, January 5, 1970.

Professor Leopold Kretzenbacher, Seminar für Deutsche und Vergleichende Volkskunde, Universität München, Munich, Germany, September 25, 1969.

5. In *Jeux Interdits* (*Forbidden Games*) a rural French boy put shells on the graves of dead animals.

6. Mircea Eliade, "Observations on the Symbolism of Shells," *Images and Symbols: Studies in Religious Symbolism*, tr. Philip Mairet (London, 1961), pp. 125-150.

7. *The Cult of the Mother Goddess: An Archeological and Documentary Study* (New York, 1959), p. 16.

8. Sir Mortimer Wheeler, "A Symbol in Ancient Times," *The Scallop: Studies of a Shell and Its Influences on Humankind*, ed. Ian Cox (London: The Shell Transport and Trading Company, Ltd., 1957), pp. 33-48.

9. *Ibid.*, p. 47.

10. Joseph Armstrong Baird, *The Churches of Mexico: 1530-1810* (Berkeley and Los Angeles, 1962), p. 84.

11. Wheeler, p. 48.

12. See note 6 above.

The Cotton Gin

By E. J. RISSMANN

BACK about 1900-10 a community in the hill country of southwest Travis County consisted, generally, of a store, a school, a church, and maybe a cotton gin. From these radiated dirt roads for ranchers and farmers to travel by horse-drawn vehicles or by walking. Time and distance governed activities. Cedar Valley, where I lived with my grandparents and parents, was a kind of center of activity for the country roundabout. Other such centers were Driftwood, Oak Hill (then Oatmanville), Bee Caves, Fitzhugh, and Dripping Springs. The latter had also a grist mill, operated by a huge wheel powered by a running spring. Oak Hill and Driftwood had the only gins, the one at Oak Hill first owned and operated by Mr. Andrew Patton and then, beginning about 1913, by Mr. Max Spillman, who later moved it to Bee Caves.

Almost every landowner or tenant farmer raised cotton, in addition to such other crops as cane, corn, oats, and milo maize. We, too, raised cotton, maybe one fourth or one fifth of a bale to the acre. We had it ginned at Driftwood, where my cousin Justus Wilhelm, later his brother Joe, owned and operated the gin. Through consultation with Mr. Max Spillman I have revived some of my recollections of this gin.

45

Justus, evidently foreseeing the times when cotton could no longer be profitably raised in these communities, moved away and established a gin at Guadalupe, Texas, a better cotton country. Joe operated the gin another few years, then went into politics, first as County Judge of Hays County, later as Mayor of San Marcos, though he still used his large ranch between Driftwood and Buda for the raising of cattle.

It was perhaps about 1910 when cotton raising began to wane in our communities, especially because of boll weevils and cotton worms. Boll weevils, members of the numerous beetle family, somehow crossed the Rio Grande from Mexico, where they had subsisted on wild and scattered cotton plants, and invaded the lush cotton lands of the south. (Not so lush, of course, in our hill country.) They waxed strong, multiplied in incredible numbers, and levied a heavy toll. The continuing emphasis on cotton growing had provided a favorable environment. That was before nature had begun to produce its checks and balances, and before the coming of man-made insecticides. The boll weevils stung the bolls, causing them to shrivel or die.

The cotton worm, like the boll weevil, was a destructive enemy of the cotton grower. It was the larva of a certain moth that traveled ever northward, but never backward, until it died with the coming of cold weather. Successive hordes of these larvae became spread over the cotton country. They defoliated the stalks. Without the green leaves with their chlorophyll there could be no production, through photosynthesis, of the plant foods needed to sustain the stalks. Consequently there could be no maturing of either blooms or bolls.

In later years, about 1920, I saw how low-flying planes spread insecticides over cotton fields in Live Oak County, and how rank the cotton grew before the dwarf varieties of still later years. I once saw cotton so tall that it was picked by men and women on horseback.

Cotton picking when I was a small boy brought together a lot of people; it was a big event. On our place it involved not only the men folks in the family, but the help of neighbors and of charcoal burners who lived in our pastures.

The cotton was picked two rows at a time. Each picker dragged a large ducking sack, fastened over his shoulder with a strap. Some pickers used gloves to keep their hands from getting sore, and some wore pads to protect their knees. The sacks full, the cotton was taken to the wagon, or wagons, to be weighed, both to determine how much each picker should receive in pay and to ascertain when the 1500 pounds had been accumulated to make a bale, which after ginning would be about 500 pounds of lint.

It was a lot of labor, the growing of a cotton crop. First the land had to be prepared, the seeds planted from a horse-drawn planter which contained in its vertical cylinder a perforated chain-operated disk to space the seeds in the furrows. After the cotton reached the height of about three inches, the spaces between the rows were plowed with a double-shovel, with two "sweeps" that made a shallow furrow, to eliminate grass and weeds and to bank the dirt against the plants. Then the cotton had to be "chopped," that is, thinned to make better stalks. Sometimes it had to be plowed and chopped a second time if the weeds and grass came back. Cotton needed plenty of heat and sunshine. The chopping was a fatiguing job; working all day in a cramped position would cause "cricks." The women wore sunbonnets that covered face and neck to save their complexions. The men, in addition to their usual garb of denim shirts and overalls, wore "jumpers" (jackets) of the same material. The jumpers hung loose, and the wind coming up under them cooled perspiring bodies. Travelers on the deserts wear turbans, veils, and robes as a protection against heat. No sun-tan faddists with bare torsos among either them or the workers in cotton fields!

When the wagon or wagons were full, they were driven to the Driftwood gin for ginning.

I remember quite well the Wilhelm gin there, a huge, two-story lumber and sheet-metal structure, and the wagons lined up waiting their turn to go under the long shed, where a telescoped, jointed, movable metal pipe known as a "sucker" sucked the cotton into the maws of the gin stands upstairs. The suction came from the steam engine that operated the gin. Upstairs the cotton passed first through the "cleaner" to remove excess leaves and other waste. Then it fell into the gin stands, where saws and brushes separated the lint from the seeds. The brushes created enough breeze to blow the lint into a press lined with coarse bagging to cover the completed bale. The seed dropped into a sort of trough, through which it traveled either on a conveyor belt or along an auger into a huge box with a trap door at the bottom for emptying into the wagon below.

When enough lint was accumulated in the press for a 500-pound bale, the bale was moved to the edge of a platform, securely fastened together with metal ties, and either shunted down a ramp to the ground or lowered with a windlass into the wagon. Some farmers left their bales in the yard for storage, and others hauled them home for the same purpose, until the market price was favorable. Most took the seed along for cow feed and for next year's planting. A few left it to apply on the usual fee of about $5.00 for ginning. If the farmer did not want to take home all of his seed, he left the remainder at the gin, some of it occasionally to be used as fuel for the steam engine—it made a quick and hot fire. During the time when I knew the Wilhelm gin it was powered by a huge steam engine sunk in a pit and fueled with cordwood. A wide belt running from the engine's huge flywheel turned shafts and pulleys, which activated other belts to run the gin machinery. And who can ever forget the smell of steam, or forget the clouds of smoke that rose from the gin's huge smokestack!

In the years when I knew this gin, cotton seed was not yet being manufactured into cotton seed "cake" and hulls for cattle feed, nor was cotton seed oil being widely used in the manufacture of household shortenings.

The cotton bales were usually marketed in Austin, where they were run through compresses to reduce their size for rail shipment. The price received by the farmer was perhaps 6¢ or 7¢ a pound. It was about 1914, I think, when there was a "buy a bale" movement to increase the price to 10¢. World War I caused the price to go up. It was not until about 1920 that cotton reached a price, according to Mr. Spillman, of 20¢ a pound. The "buy a bale" movement may have been during the 1921 depression, when all prices were low. I can't be sure, as my memory fails me.

Cotton was the "cash crop" of our communities in the period I remember best, 1900-10. It brought in the cash to make available the things that only money could buy. My father, of course, had additional ways "to make a dollar." His versatility in carpentry, blacksmithing, and stone masonry brought him dollars in working for neighbors. Also, he was successful in the raising of horses, cattle, and hogs. There was some revenue too from the sale of wood and from the charcoal burners on the place. In addition he had a good garden to provide his family with fresh vegetables.

What the noon hour brought at the Wilhelm gin is something to remember. A sharp blast from the gin's whistle announced that it was twelve o'clock or that the last bale before twelve had been completed. Farmers and gin hands, who had got up before daylight, retreated to the shade to eat lunches of biscuit or lightbread with some kind of meat and to discuss the economics of the world. Then some dozed or pitched horseshoes. Boys sometimes played "mumble-peg" with their pocket knives or catch with a baseball.

Sometimes children would come with their fathers to the gin. To while away the time they would run races, ride stick horses, or watch insects. In the watching of insects, the doodlebug was the favorite, the ogre that lived in small craters of sand or loose soil. The doodlebug is the larva of a slow-moving, four-winged fly. It lives at the bottom of the doodlebug hole and uses strategy and camouflage to catch its prey, usually an unwary ant that blunders into the pit and slides down the embankment. The doodlebug sends up a sudden shower of particles to confuse the ant, and then nabs him with its calipers. Another name for the doodlebug is "ant lion." The children liked to tease doodlebugs into action. With a twig or stem of grass they would stir the dry, loose dirt of the miniature crater and chant:

> Doodlebug, doodlebug,
> Fly away home.
> Your house is on fire,
> And your children will burn.
> Doodlebug, doodlebug,
> Fly away home.

It was fun to watch other bugs too, the tumblebug rolling his sphere of dung or the carrier beetle summoned from afar by his acute sense of smell to feed on any dead animal. If dusk came before father's bale was ginned, there were fireflies to watch, but by this time the children would probably be asleep, tired out.

Cotton raising and cotton gins exist no more in these hill country communities. The land is too unproductive. The fields have become grazing land or they grow feed for cattle. Cattle raising and deer leases have replaced cotton as a source of cash. The land, now heavily taxed, is being sold off in small tracts to city people who want to move to the country. It is too expensive to hold. And most country people have jobs in town. Few of the present generation know about cotton gins and what went on in and around them during ginning time.

Log Cabins
To Sunday Houses

By ESTHER L. MUELLER

O N Friday evening, May 8, 1846, a hundred and twenty Germans stood on the red clay bank of a creek in central Texas, looking across into an oak grove.[1] Here they were to build a town named Fredericksburg. Behind them lay the Atlantic crossing (made under the sponsorship of the Society for the Protection of German Emigrants in Texas), also a stay at Indianola and New Braunfels, and finally a sixteen-day trek from New Braunfels to this point. As their worldly goods were unloaded from twenty Mexican carts, sight of the single log cabin across the creek must have stirred desire for the homes they hoped to build.

Surveyors had set up the cabin and left it, after laying out town blocks and a main street named San Saba Strasse. Some years from now the emigrants hoped to follow it west into a San Saba grant provided for them.

Commissioner-General John L. Meusebach, after seeing the hordes of Comanches wintering there, bought land near the Pedernales River for their immediate home, naming it Fredericksburg for Prince Frederick of Prussia.[2] When some years later the settlers acquired titles to their land grants, most of them sold their claims,

By now they had received town lots and ten-acre plots at Fredericksburg. Many were preempting land in Gillespie County. Hardship, privations, and a need for neighbors had woven strong ties. Fredericksburg had become home.

In 1846, before the distribution of town lots, they had erected brush arbors and stretched linen sheets on the bank of Baron's Creek. Surveyor Bene had named the stream after Baron von Meusebach. In folk talk, though, this source of water for drinking, washing, and swimming became "Stadt-crick."

By summer the population reached five hundred. Some settlers lived in dirt-floored, one-room cabins built of poles rammed into the earth and roofed with oak shakes or grass. Many were still in brush shelters when the first norther struck, but a year later the majority were living in half-timbered (*Fachwerk*) houses.

In 1846 the United States and Mexico went to war and the transportation of supplies dwindled. Food became scarce. To other problems were added germs of a pestilence that a year before had brought death to hundreds of immigrants at Indianola and New Braunfels. At Fredericksburg they called it "the cholera." The commissary had no medicine to combat it. A colonist wrote back to Germany that people died like gnats.[3] As the epidemic spread, in some instances all members of a family living in a log hut died, one after another. By November over ninety persons had been buried in the cemetery plot near the creek. There had been no minister at their burials.

Survivors grieved all the more for having no pastor or priest to condole with them. Morale was revived when in December an immigrant train brought a Protestant pastor, the Reverend Henry S. W. Basse, and his family. Although the pastor found hardship, illness, confusion, and dissent among the settlers, he organized a Protestant congregation at once.[4] Shortly afterward John Leyendecker arrived and served the Catholics as lay preacher.

By New Year the settlers, already suffering from malnutrition, feared the future. Horses and cattle were starving too, for all grass in the vicinity of Fredericksburg had been burned. No one knew the cause of the fires, but the settlers blamed the Indians. To ease their fear, John O. Meusebach visited the Comanches in their winter hunting ground early in 1847 and made a peace treaty with them.[5] The Indians now brought deer meat and skins filled with honey and bear fat to trade with the settlers.

Indians watched too in June 1847 as a cornerstone was laid for a community church in the middle of San Saba Strasse between Market and Courthouse Squares. Eventually massive oak beams arose for an octagonal-shaped building. An eight-sided cupola made a belfry above the roof, while on top a weathervane turned with the wind. Erected for all religious denominations, the building served also as an early schoolhouse. Because its rounded shape resembled a certain type of coffee grinder in use then, the settlers called it "die Kaffemühle."[6] Cherished through the years, it became for many the symbol of Fredericksburg.

Its bell rang at six o'clock on Saturday evening with the invitation that the church bells in Germany had given them, to come to church on Sunday. By 1864, when three new steeples were outlined against the sky, four bells rang out their invitations together.

On occasion the bell in the Vereinskirche rang alone, as on the night of February 1, 1864, when masked men appeared at the home of Louis Schuetze, village teacher near the Market Square. He had often and openly proclaimed loyalty to the Union. As they dragged him out of his home, his daughter ran screaming to the bell of the Vereinskirche. The armed party that gathered searched all night.[7] Next morning they found him, hanged on an oak tree. Dr. William Keidel, who treated both Unionists and Confederates, compared local conditions in a letter to his brother in Germany, to those of the French Revolution.[8]

When Gillespie County was created in 1848, young Dr. Keidel led a group to settle on the Pedernales. The Indians were friendly, especially to the doctor, who treated their ailments. Often Indians visiting at the Jacob Roeder home while the family was at church played tricks, such as taking all knives and forks from the kitchen, bending the soft-tined forks into fantastic shapes, then hiding all cutlery in a hollow tree.

During the Civil War, however, the Indians were no longer playful. By this time over three hundred families were farming in Gillespie County, some near town, others in widely separated, lonely areas. Now the Indians not only stole horses, but murdered their owners too. Even with Rangers in the county and soldiers often at

Fort Martin Scott, between 1861 and 1870 Indians killed nine persons and took two children captive in scattered areas of Gillespie County.

In spite of their uneasiness, rural families were up at dawn, working all day, plowing, planting, or harvesting, always clearing and enclosing new fields with fences of zig-zag rail, picket posts, or most often with limestone rock. After a time they left their cabins for limestone houses.

Their great problem—loneliness—remained constant. Letters were few, visitors rare. For days on end members of the family saw no one except one another. Sometimes, gathered about the supper table at evening devotions, they heard human voices outside, imitating the hoot of an owl or the scream of a panther, but unless the horses became disturbed, they ignored their Indian visitors.

In their isolation they treasured the ties with relatives and friends in town. When they came to town on Saturday, they brought gifts for their hosts—sausages, dried venison, butter, cheese, ham, or vegetables. Catholics, going to Saturday mass, arrived first, the Protestants by afternoon. When twilight came early, storekeepers did business by lamp or candle light. Everyone understood that the farmers came to town on Saturday to be there for church on Sunday morning.

The largest of the Protestant churches was the Evangelical congregation, to whom the Emigration Society had deeded the Vereinskirche. During the years the congregation had laid a wooden floor over the uneven stones, ceiled off massive overhead beams, and provided benches with backs. Relatives crowded these benches on Palm Sunday of 1874, when forty-nine candidates for confirmation appeared. Twenty-five girls wore white dresses with colored ribbon sashes; twenty-four boys, new suits. After confirmation rites had made them members of the congregation, they were honored at special dinners. In 1886, however, friction over the name and constitution of the church caused a split.[9] Two new Protestant congregations emerged, and each built a church of its own. By 1893, the Vereinskirche, now the property of the county, stood deserted in the middle of Main Street.

Three years later the old church became briefly again the symbol of Fredericksburg. It was May of 1896. For three days the townsmen celebrated the fiftieth anniversary of the founding of Fredericksburg. The Vereinskirche, with mortar and rock removed from its walls, had become a pavilion. A new wooden floor covered the old. Massive beams were cleaned and polished, and the heavy posts were wrapped with garlands of cedar. As the band played under its roof, old settlers lingered there recalling the days when this landmark was their church and schoolhouse. At dusk when the town's new electric lights came on, crowds gathered there again and danced far into the night.

They cherished the old Kaffeemühle all the more for knowing that it was doomed. It had been pronounced a traffic hazard, there in the middle of the street, and a public nuisance, for as it stood empty village cows had broken down its doors and taken shelter inside. Yet so strong was sentiment against its demolition that a year later no one had made a bid for the job. However, by August of 1897, the bid was made, the court accepted it, and the Vereinskirche was razed. After it was gone—and almost simultaneously with its disappearance—something strange and new came into the life of Fredericksburg, the Sunday house.

With it came a new era that developed as swiftly as if everyone had been waiting for it, an era of the Sunday houses that lasted approximately half a century. No one knows who built the first one. It is said that when there came to one man's ears a suggestion that the Sunday visits of his family were no longer welcome to relatives, he vowed to build himself a Sunday house, and the idea became popular.[10]

Miss Julia Estill, who in 1923 mentioned Sunday houses in an article on German customs in Gillespie County, said of them, "They may be found almost anywhere in Fredericksburg; on Main Street nestling comfortably against the village smithy; in the fashionable suburbs beside a modern bungalow."[11]

The German immigrants who first cleared away brush and rocks for small fields had no dream of Sunday houses. It was their sons, born in Texas, who later built them. During the Civil War while the fathers were fighting for the Confederacy, or for the Union, or perhaps evading conscription for a cause they rejected, their sons shared at home in the responsibilities of a man. They studied at country schools, but their religious instruction came from a Catholic priest or a Lutheran or Methodist minister at Fredericksburg. As family heads later, they were staunchly faithful to the doctrines of their churches.

John Metzger, who in 1898 built one of the earliest Sunday houses, liked being in easy walking distance of his church, so he bought a lot only a block from the Catholic Church.[12] When lots were available, others did likewise, and here and there in town Sunday houses clustered near the churches. John Metzger was born in a dirt-floored log cabin in 1849. Three years later he watched his father and grandfather building a rock house with wooden floors and a great stone chimney. But he built his two-room Sunday house of lumber, painting it white and adding modern gingerbread trim. He included a transitional feature; as in the early *Fachwerk* house, the attic above the front room was reached by an outside stairway. He dug a well near the kitchen and fenced the lot. The fence was a necessity, for cows roamed the streets until the town became a city in 1932.

As other Sunday houses appeared, each builder considered his needs. If his family lived near town and used a Sunday house only for Sunday dinner, a one-room lumber house sufficed. Sometimes, for the sake of geniality, he added a front porch. Occasionally an abandoned *Fachwerk* or limestone house was renovated with plaster and whitewash into a comfortable Sunday house.

Large families who traveled fifteen or twenty miles to town in a wagon or hack liked the two-story lumber house that had two rooms downstairs and a large room or two above. The long, shaded porch with its decorative trim encouraged sociability. Here the family often stayed overnight for "second day" services. And if their church did not frown heavily on dancing, the entire family might attend the second holiday dance at a hall in town.

A Sunday house was compact, yet uncluttered. Its furnishings consisted of essentials. Most important was the cast-iron stove. The table with its backless benches was almost as necessary. A cupboard well filled with dishes, glasses, grocery staples, dish towels, candles and matches, and, of course, cutlery, was desirable. The dishpan, the washbasin and pitcher, and the water bucket with a dipper were all necessities. A rocking chair and a folding cot made the stay more relaxing. In the two-story Sunday house, there was room for beds, supplemented by a stack of pallets and pillows, and a washstand and bureau upstairs.

If the two-story house was crowded with children and their parents, the adults ate first while the children played outside. But long before the parents were ready to leave their talking, the children were back, nudging their mothers, letting them know that they were hungry too. When the men had finally moved to the front porch, the children sat down for "zweiter Tisch."

In this type of house grandparents hoped some day to make a new home. Julia Estill, picturing this transition, wrote, "Later, when the farmer is a-weary of labor in the fields, and has a plump little bank account all his own, he and his faithful wife, who had helped him accumulate this wealth by practicing thrift and economy, leave the old home to their son, and come to town to spend a peaceful old age in the Sunday house to which, perhaps, a room or two and a little front porch have been added."[13]

At the Sunday house one shared a wealth of family living, at times exhilarating, tiring, joyful, or sad. Families, at their Sunday houses on the Saturday before Easter, enjoyed watching the Easter bonfires blaze on the hills about town after dark. Occasionally six, seven, or more flamed against the sky. Small children saw Easter rabbits dyeing eggs in the hills. And great-grandparents might recall dances around such fires in the hills of Hessen[14] or Westphalia, dances which their parents called pagan.

During Lent when instruction was intensified for the catechumens, a grandmother or older sister stayed with them in town, helping them study by coal-oil lamp. Protestants were confirmed on Palm Sunday; Catholics, on Easter Sunday. For the celebration of these occasions, the choicest food and the best of silver and linen were brought to the Sunday houses where relatives gathered to honor them.

Sunday houses were useful for the weekday too. Whether the family was in town to shop or visit the County Fair, the Sunday house was like a home. Sometimes when a member of the family was ill and needed a doctor's care, he was brought to the Sunday house and one of the family stayed with him. In early days funeral services were held at the home of the deceased. When a grandfather who had died in the country was to be buried in the cemetery in town, his Sunday house was the proper place for services. Then a long line of buggies and hacks carrying relatives, neighbors, and friends, followed a hearse over a winding country road to the Sunday house. Services were conducted in the front room, where the casket stood, but since the room was small, mourners filled the yard until they joined the procession moving toward the cemetery. Through all of these services the Sunday houses endeared themselves to the families that visited them.

Yet the end of the Sunday-house era was inevitable, even before it began. The first settlers of Fredericksburg, most of whom had traveled by train to reach their port of embarkation at Bremerhaven or Antwerp, must have recognized, as they trudged on foot from New Braunfels to Fredericksburg, the value of good roads and comfortable transportation. It was eventually the automobile and the new paved roads that made the Sunday house unnecessary to their descendants.

When the first Sunday houses appeared, new hacks, buggies, and surreys were replacing the old covered wagons. The time was far removed from the day when a man took his sack of wheat on a travois to Guenther's Mill on the Live Oak. Soon the farmer, coming to town on Sunday and stopping his hack at the west corner of the Market Square to water his horses at the wooden troughs, looked speculatively, enviously, after the neighbor who passed by in an automobile.

By the outbreak of World War II, country living had been so improved with electricity in the home and paved roads to town, that after Sunday morning church services the rural family drove back to the ranch home for Sunday dinner, without a stop at the Sunday house. Gas rationing in wartime, however, brought hacks, surreys, and buggies back to Main Street. With it, life in the Sunday house became again as warm and friendly as it had ever been.

Today Sunday-house living has run its course. The houses themselves have met a kinder fate. Of the more than a hundred Sunday houses that once quickened the life of Fredericksburg, a few have been razed. A few stand vacant, but still intact. The others, remodeled now, are surrounded by green lawns and pecan-tree shade. Having served the purpose for which they were intended, they have become the homes of lively families who occupy them every day.

NOTES

1. Robert Penninger, *Fest-Ausgabe zum fünfzig-jährigen Jubilaum der deutschen Kolonie Friedericksburg* (Fredericksburg: Arwed Hillman, 1896), p. 62.

2. Irene Marschall King, *John O. Meusebach, German Colonizer in Texas* (Austin: University of Texas Press, 1967), p. 73.

3. A. Kriegar to Cappes, Oct. 1, 1846, in *Archiv der fürstlichen Standesherrschaft Solms-Braunfels*, XLIII, 63. Transcribed in German.

4. *Pioneers in God's Hills: A History of Fredericksburg and Gillespie County: People and Events* (Austin: Von Boeckmann-Jones Co., 1960), p. 6. This is a collaborative work.

5. Moritz Tiling, *History of the German Element in Texas from 1820-1850* (Houston: M. Tiling, 1913), pp. 94-104.

6. Rudolph Leopold Biesele, *The History of the German Settlements in Texas, 1831-1861* (Austin: Von Boeckmann-Jones Co., 1930) p. 143.

7. *Pioneers*, p. 188.

8. *Pioneers*, p. 84.

9. O. E. Lindenberg, *Holy Ghost Lutheran Church* (Fredericksburg: Radio Post, 1949). This booklet gives the details of the split in the Vereinskirche.

10. Esther Mueller, "Sunday Houses of Fredericksburg," *Texas Monthly*, April 1930, p. 346.

11. Julia Estill, "Customs Among the German Descendants of Gillespie County," *Coffee in the Gourd*, Publications of the Texas Folklore Society, II (1923), 68.

12. *Pioneers*, p. 134.

13. Estill, p. 69.

14. See Sir James Frazer, *The Golden Bough* (abgd. ed.; London: Macmillan, 1951), p. 712.

Black Easter:
April 14, 1935

By SILVIA GRIDER

EYEWITNESS ACCOUNTS

WHILE Hoovervilles beckoned and Dorothea Lang photographed the exodus of the Oakies, in the Texas Panhandle weather reports daily reminded the grim populace of "high winds accompanied by blowing dust and limited visibility." By 1935 the "Great American Desert" was a parched reality. Stretching from Colorado to Kansas, through Oklahoma to the Texas Panhandle, the Dust Bowl was choking on the thick, powdery dust which had, when it used to rain, produced crops too abundant for the overloaded grain elevators and cotton gins. Drought and depression combined to wreck this fertile and benign land.

The Panhandle town of Pampa squatted on the edge of this seeming pastoral Armageddon and its hardy oilfield boomtown residents watched the parched Caprock wind exact its daily toll of their soil, their energy, and their meager wealth. Hitler had not yet marched on Poland, but the concept of *blitzkreig* ground itself into the Pampa consciousness as its people ran for shelter from the hot, abrasive, and unexpected assaults of the dust-laden wind.

61

Nevertheless, Pampans weren't ready yet to pull up stakes and head for California. Dalhart, their neighbor to the northwest, briefly became the national Dust Bowl symbol when an impoverished pair of crows built their nest in a dead tree from scraps of barbed wire—the wind had long since blown away all other building materials.[1] Pampans laughed over this product of the hard times and went on to tell each other their own stories of death from dust pneumonia, wheat sprouts electrocuted by dust-generated static, and how upon awakening in the morning one could see the white impression of his face on the dusty pillow case. The Dust Bowl attained local immortality for them on a quiet, clear Palm Sunday afternoon.

Sunday dawned clear and windless, without a speck of haze. From the rise just the other side of White Deer the grain elevator was barely visible on the horizon, nearly ten miles distant. It was as in the good old days before anybody ever heard of dusters. The morning lazied itself away in church-going and chicken-frying and reading the funnies. After lunch everybody in town was out and stirring around.

The Jess Turners and another couple headed over toward the Hayhook Ranch for some sightseeing. Charlie Pipes and his wife Violet were on his regular police beat, checking downtown to see if all the stores were locked. But on this afternoon Charlie was getting a headstart so he and Violet could get on with celebrating her birthday. She was wearing the white dress Charlie had given her which, as it turned out, was never fit to wear again. Things were kinda slow at Minnie's Cafe, so Sid Maples was mostly shooting the bull, with a little cooking and dish washing on the side. Will Rogers was playing in the popular *Life Begins at Forty* at the old Lanora Theater, where R. C. Grider was doorman.

The Big Black One gave no warning. From Amarillo to Miami eighty miles northeast, as though of one accord, people's amazed glances swung to the north as a ground-hugging, rolling black cloudbank of incredible density and height bore down on them. There was no sound, no wind, no preceding dust—only a swirling wall of blackness that blotted out the sun and threw a shroud of emulsified dust over everything. Most people stood transfixed and watched it hit. Some swore at first it was the smoke of a huge prairie fire;

others, a freak cold front moving in. But almost universal was the anxiety that this, here and on a quiet Sunday afternoon, might be the end of the world.

Churning along at fifty miles an hour, the duster pounced on the startled spectators. The town temporarily dissolved in near panic and confusion. Those who had storm cellars ran for them, fearing that a tornado might be hot on the heels of this monstrosity. Past experience with dust storms drove others to a frenzy of window shutting and door slamming. Sheets were snatched from clothes lines and beds and wetted down in hopes of controlling the dust. Within minutes everything stopped but the wind. As "Preacher" McKenzie put it, "We were too scared to pray and too scared to run; we were more interested in breathing."[2]

Sunday drivers out on the highway tried to outrun the cloud and beat it to town; few made it. The dust engulfed them all and those who literally rode out the storm in their cars leave behind descriptions of how it got "black as night," and "you couldn't see your hand in front of your face." They all pulled off the roads and waited for the storm to let up because it was impossible to see to drive in the swirling dust; headlights were useless because they were invisible only a few feet away. Many of these unfortunates ended up walking back to town that night because the powdery dust and static electricity in the air had stalled their cars.

The occupants of one of those stalled cars were the Jess Turners, out on the Hayhook Ranch. The story, as Jess tells it, is this:

White Deer Creek had a high north bank and we had climbed down under there to sit and talk. As the sun was getting low, we decided to go before it got dark. We climbed up the bank and suddenly there we were walking north in plain view of the duster. It was 5,000 feet high and rolling on the ground. My wife thought that the whole world was afire. We ran about fifty yards and made it to the car just as it hit.

We couldn't see each other or the steering wheel for about thirty minutes. The sand caused static in the air. The cars [there were at least two in the party] grounded out and wouldn't start and we ended up running the batteries down too.

It was nightfall by then and really dark. The girls were scared, so we decided to try to find the ranch house, which we knew was by the creek. So we stayed on the north bank and started walking. It was dark and there was lots of brush. We finally came to a cow crossing and took off our shoes and waded across.

We kept on following that winding creek looking for the ranch house. We bumped into the barn in the dark. I was so lost and turned around I didn't feel right about directions. When we found the picket fence and the gate we went right in to the camp house. It was fully stocked with supplies. There was a little sign which said, "If you come along, fix a bite to eat, but wash the dishes." We all tried to wash up. Our faces were black as any nigger. It looked like pencil marks down to the chin where the tears ran. Tom Cooper took the carburetor off his car and washed it with gasoline from the tractor and got his car started.[3]

B. G. Gordon had just bought a new '35 Chevy and was out breaking it in, over toward White Deer. He says, "I saw what appeared to be a real low cloud in the northwest. I realized it was rolling, tumbling. I tried to get back to town before it did, but it caught us in the car by the old *News* building. We just sat in the car until it began to ease up. It got so dark you couldn't see the people in the car."[4]

Likewise, in town, there was nothing to do but sit and wait to see what would happen. Residents were accustomed to poking wet wadded newspaper into the cracks between window sills and around doors and also to covering their faces with wet rags to make breathing easier. But there were still other problems. For example, there was a houseful of kids at the Methodist parsonage in White Deer, and to keep them calmed down the preacher's wife decided to get them all something to eat. She always kept plenty in the ice box for just such occasions. She got out a big jello and whipped-cream dessert, but before anybody could touch a bite of it the whole thing was covered with what looked like black powdered sugar.[5]

The dust in the theater boiling out through the air conditioning ducts looked so much like smoke that some patrons thought the theater was on fire. Hearing the hubbub outside and smelling the dust, most of the moviegoers got up and left. Matt Jennings had parked his car directly across the street from the theater or he would have never found it by just groping around in the murk. To add to the confusion, just for a joke, some guys got out on Cuyler Street and started hog calling; their disembodied voices were carried for blocks by the wind.[6]

Carl Benefiel, the manager of the Lanora, had a new movie "rig."

Seeing the chance to make a real historical document, he grabbed the camera and tripod and ran out in front of the theater to get it set up. He had just gotten the camera adjusted and focused as the cloud rolled overhead and blacked out everything.[7]

The worst part of the storm lasted only about thirty minutes, although visibility was limited to six miles or less for fifty-five hours, one of the longest spans on record.[8] After about three hours the wind died down and people started to dig out. Wherever windows had been left open, cleaning up had to be done with scoops and shovels. The Electrolux sweeper people did a "land office business." By the next morning the powdery, greasy dust, as fine as if it had been sifted through silk, was settling and the whole duster was on its way to becoming just another tall Texas tale.

THE PATTERN

Thirty-five years later, this is still the archtypal storm against which Pampans measure all others. The only other individual duster that they ever mention is "Big Red" of 1923. All the rest are lumped together as "they"—*they* came blowing in nearly every day before noon, *they* filled the sky so that one could look safely straight into the sun, *they* ruined laundry and made housekeeping impossible.

Although some facts and details have become hazy with time, the general reaction after the event is similar to that evoked by other such unexpected disasters as Pearl Harbor, the assassination of President Kennedy, or the New York City Blackout. People will relate such details as what they were doing and who they were with when the duster struck. Such minutiae as the clothes worn at the time or radio programs being listened to are also mentioned. When people are asked about the Dust Bowl in general or this storm in particular, the typical response is nearly always a description following a stylized pattern and idiom.

1. *The date.* Although many people recall the date exactly, others at least get it approximately, such as "in the spring of '34 or '35 or thereabouts." This storm is a point of reference for other events. Most people remember that it hit on a Sunday afternoon about 3:00 or 4:00 p. m., which is curious because the newspaper

records that the storm struck at 6:45.[9] Perhaps the discrepancy lies in the long daylight hours in the spring that may have made it seem earlier than it actually was. Although in reality it was Palm Sunday, the later newspaper accounts are responsible for the nickname of Black Easter. On March 4, the week after Easter, Amarillo experienced its worst duster and it, too, is sometimes referred to as Black Easter. Some papers also referred to the storm as the Black Blizzard, although it was not cold at all.

2. *First sight of the cloud.* The descriptions of the cloud as it came up on the horizon are remarkably similar. People say that the cloud was big and black, rolling and pitching, and hugging the ground. They also designate it as coming out of the north or northwest. People apparently don't intentionally try to exaggerate their descriptions of what the cloud looked like; they resort to metaphors, clichés, and hand gestures for lack of any other means of conveying the impression this storm left with them.

3. *What happened when it hit.* Recollections become highly individualized and varied at this point because each person interviewed tells exactly what he was doing against the background of the storm. Still, many of the descriptive phrases are recurrent. The most common are "black as night," "black as the inside of a hat," "couldn't see your hand in front of your face," or "pitch black." Other people resort to religious metaphor such as "black as when Jesus was hanging on the cross," a concept directly related to the fact that the storm struck during the Easter season.

4. *Results of the storm.* Many of the favorite anecdotes are probably apocryphal, especially those about miraculous religious conversions experienced during the storm. Stories abound of people falling to their knees and praying for deliverance, but none of these have as of yet been documented by a participant or a witness. Most people end up their stories of the duster by telling about some of the problems they encountered during the cleaning-up process, such as how deep the dust was, how long it took to get it all swept out, etc. Others like to tell of the out-of-the-way places

The big storm rolls into Pampa.

where they found dust, such as inside light bulbs and ice boxes, or in the crankcases of their cars.

NEWSPAPERS, HISTORIES, PICTURES, AND A SONG

Although the oral recollections of those who were there are the most common source of information about this duster, there are other accounts equally valuable and interesting. In recent years the duster has become a favorite topic for interview transcripts being placed in the archives of the West Texas State University Museum and Library in Canyon. The drought of the middle and late '50's produced a few mild but unpleasant dusters, which prompted many a comparison by local residents with those of twenty years before. Newspaper features abounded, the best ones appearing in the *Amarillo Globe News.* [10]

The *Pampa Daily News* and the *Amarillo Globe News* provide the only contemporary published accounts of the storm.[11] Many who are interviewed now qualify their remarks with, "There was a piece in the paper about that," and a quick check in the news archives usually confirms this. There are also a few published accounts of the storm and some photographs in local county histories.[12] The statistical records of the United States Weather Bureau in Amarillo are significant for the data they have recorded regarding wind velocity and visibility during the dust storms on a day-to-day, year-by-year basis.[13]

The most popular souvenirs of the Black Duster were snapshots printed up and sold in sets by the Wirshing Studio in Pampa. Roy Holt, for example, stood out in his back yard and snapped pictures with the family Kodak until the dirt covered him. The specks of dirt that blew onto the lens are clearly visible in the prints. Irl Smith took similar pictures of the dust cloud with a borrowed box camera as it rolled over the farm where he and his wife were visiting in Groom. Mr. Smith, who was then working at Fred's Studio, says that Fred acquired the best negatives that people brought in to have developed and printed pictures from them by the hundreds to sell to souvenir seekers, who queued up half way down the block to purchase a set of twelve for one dollar.[14] Some residents still have prints of these pictures and show them off proudly as they tell about their experiences with the storm. One of these pictures was finally published in the local newspaper, the *Pampa Daily News,* on May 8, 1935.

The literary tradition of Black Easter is not limited, however, to newspaper and weather-bureau reports and amateur snapshots. The late Woody Guthrie immortalized this day when he wrote a song, one version of which begins,

> I'll sing this song but I'll sing it again
> Of the place that I lived on the West Texas Plains.
> In the city of Pampa, the county of Gray,
> Here's what all of the good people there say,
> So long, it's been good to know you. . . .15

Woody, who was married and living in Pampa in 1935, watched that storm roll in, as he says, "like the Red Sea closing in on the Israel children."16 From then on his story is the same as hundreds of others told by people who were there that day—how inside his little "dwelling house" it got so black "you couldn't see your hand in front of your face" and how a burning light bulb looked no brighter than a lighted cigarette. However, contrary to what Woody says in the Library of Congress recording with Alan Lomax and the verses of the song itself, he and his wife were getting ready as usual to go to church with Jeff and Aleen Guthrie the afternoon of April 14th.17 Jeff and Aleen hadn't come by yet when the storm struck, so Woody and Mary rode it out at home in their little shotgun shack at 420 S. Russell and never made it to church. Nobody got out to go anywhere that night. In looking back, Mary reflects now that neither of them was scared, nor did they think or talk about the world coming to an end right then. They certainly received no telephone calls on that subject, because they had no phone. The dust was so bad that their main concern was how uncomfortable they were and how hard it was to breathe.

Woody wrote *So Long* much later, maybe even two or three years after that dusty night. Mary says that he sat at the typewriter what seemed like all the time during those last years in Pampa and during that period wrote many of his early songs, none of which became popular until he moved to New York City. *So Long* is Woody's composite version of the tales people told and made up after the duster.

It provided a convenient vehicle for his philosophizing about the possible end of the world and how people would react to it.

From Pampa the restless Woody drifted west to California and joined with the Oakies out of choice and curiosity rather than necessity. They had a sorrow and a resoluteness that he accepted as his own, and he told their story so articulately that he became an integral part of it himself. And, as with so many events that he sang about, he made Black Easter of 1935 and the other Panhandle dusters known to a worldwide audience which will be forever in his debt. But with or without the benefit of Woody's ballads, that storm has nevertheless woven itself so deeply into the folk fabric of Pampa that even now, whenever the town motto is mentioned, "Where the wheat grows and oil flows," oldtimers add grimly, "and the dust blows," and their minds turn once again to that single day which for them will make the Dust Bowl live forever.

NOTES

1. *Amarillo Globe News*, June 16, 1943.

2. E. C. McKenzie to Sylvia Grider, April 7, 1969, Monroe, La.

3. Jess Turner to Sylvia Grider, June 8, 1968, Pampa, Texas.

4. B. G. Gordon to Sylvia Grider, June 9, 1968, Pampa, Texas.

5. Martha Robertson to Sylvia Grider, July 24, 1969, El Paso, Texas.

6. Matt Jennings to Sylvia Grider, July 23, 1969, El Paso, Texas.

7. Frank Stallings to Sylvia Grider, August 13, 1969, Pampa, Texas.

8. United States Department of Commerce, Weather Bureau, Environmental Science Services Administration, Box 4026, Amarillo, Texas.

9. *Pampa Daily News*, April 15, 1935.

10. *Amarillo Globe News*, March 11, 1962. A typical feature story of this type is the one in this issue by Herbert and Carolyn Timmons, entitled "Dusty '30's Brought Misery to Plains. . .and Library of Jokes."

11. *Pampa Daily News*, April 15-19, 1935. The *Amarillo Globe News* describes the Amarillo duster of March 4, 1935, in more detail than it does the April 14th one.

12. W. J. Morton, *Snowstorms, Dust Storms, and Horses' Tails* (Dumas, Texas: Privately Published, 1966), pp. 44-45; Mrs. Ralph Randel (ed.),

A Time to Purpose [sic] : *A Chronicle of Carson County* (Hereford, Texas: Pioneer Publishers, 1966), I, 300-302.

13. United States Weather Bureau, as in note 8 above.

14. Irl Smith to Sylvia Grider, June 9, 1968, Pampa, Texas.

15. Woody Guthrie Library of Congress Recordings, Elektra Records.

16. *Ibid.*

17. Mary Boyle to Sylvia Grider, telephone conversation, February 8, 1970. Information in this and the following paragraph all comes from this same conversation.

The Camp Meeting Sketch
In Old Southwest Humor

By BILL F. FOWLER

ON the frontier of the Old Southwest there developed an institution which is virtually unique in the history of religion—the camp meeting. The first recorded mention of camp meetings indicates that they were not of extensive occurrence prior to 1800.[1] They spread throughout the Old Southwest during the first half of the nineteenth century and they were a significant factor in determining the kind of religion endemic to that region even today. For the most part, the camp meeting filled a great need for religious worship, training, and fellowship on the frontier, and in addition the vigorous religious sects which adopted the camp meeting found it an excellent means for recruiting converts to their churches. A very fiery, unsophisticated, and forceful evangelistic delivery reminiscent of Jonathan Edwards, George Whitefield, and John Wesley was the predominant style of preaching. The meetings were held in the woods or countryside; they generally lasted three to five days; sermons sometimes continued throughout the day and even throughout the night, and at large meetings several might be going on at once; and attendance was frequently phenomenal (reports of from three to twenty thousand came from participants in the Kentucky and Tennessee camp meetings of 1800 and 1801).[2]

Many of those who attended came not to worship but to find entertainment; some came only to ridicule and disrupt the meetings. Such a mixture of motives and personalities contributed to the confusion which characterized many early camp meetings, but even after they had been made more orderly through better organization, the extreme excitement caused by highly emotional sermons and songs created an atmosphere at times almost dionysiac in temper. The screams, tremblings, jerks, holy dances, fallings, and comas—seizures of all sorts—occasionally reached epidemic proportions; instances of open and clandestine promiscuity in the name of a misguided sense of Christian fellowship and love were also not unknown. Although such excesses are not the definitive characteristics of frontier religion, they did become notorious throughout the country. James B. Finley, a frontier preacher of considerable note who was not hostile to camp meetings, gives the following account of his first camp meeting experience—it was the famous Cane Ridge, Kentucky, camp meeting of 1801:

> A vast crowd, supposed by some to have amounted to twenty-five thousand, was collected together. The noise was like the roar of Niagara. The vast sea of human beings seemed to be agitated as if by a storm. I counted seven ministers, all preaching at one time, some on stumps, others on wagons. . . . Some of the people were singing, others praying, some crying for mercy in the most piteous accents, while others were shouting most vociferously. . . . A strange supernatural power seemed to pervade the entire mass of mind collected there. . . .
> I stepped up onto a log, where I could have a better view of the surging sea of humanity. The scene that then presented itself to my mind was indescribable. At one time I saw at least five hundred swept down in a moment, and then immediately followed shrieks and shouts that rent the very heavens. . . . I fled for the woods a second time, and wished I had staid at home.[3]

Most circuit riders thought of camp meetings as a means of salvation for a sinful world. Bishop Asbury described them as "The Battle axe and weapon of war. . . [which] will break down the walls of wickedness, [the] forts of hell."[4]

But many reactions to camp meeting excesses were decidedly hostile. William Porter, editor of the major humorous magazine of the mid-century—*The Spirit of the Times*—thought of camp meetings devotees as the "dregs" of society, and he called them "half-crazy zealots."[5] In view of his hostility to camp meeting excesses, it is not surprising that much of the Old Southwest humor in his magazine utilized the camp meeting as a setting for riotous humor.

This paper will examine three camp meeting sketches by Porter's contributors, with a view toward discovering common attitudes and values underlying their humor. The humor in these sketches is representative of the fantastically exaggerative humor made famous in the tall tale, but the subject matter of these sketches more clearly reveals an underlying attitude toward life common to Old Southwest humor. The common denominator of this segment of frontier literature is one which is insistent upon the value of common sense and a buoyant good humor in facing the trials and tribulations of the world, and it is noteworthy that values such as these are essentially the same as those we find in recognizably characteristic Americans such as Franklin, Paine, Jefferson, Lincoln, and Twain.

In Johnson J. Hooper's sketch entitled "Simon Suggs Attends a Camp Meeting,"[6] we meet the indomitable old fox Simon Suggs, captain of the Tallapoosy Volunteers, on one of his frequent forays into the country in search of entertainment, excitement, and replenishment for his pocketbook. In this particular instance he finds all three located in the hollow square of an encampment filled with people listening to the midday sermons and exhortations of the half-dozen preachers who were dispensing the gospel to the souls attending the Sandy Creek camp meeting. The scene which met Simon's eyes merits repetition here, for although it bears much by way of descriptive detail which might be construed as gross exaggeration, it really contains little which is not to be found repeatedly in the more objective firsthand descriptions of camp meetings from reputable sources. It is true that the humor of the sketch derives largely from exaggeration, but the exaggeration is not a result of the distortion of events but rather of the concentration of so many ludicrous events into one scene. This is Hooper's description:

> The excitement was intense. Men and women rolled about on the ground, or lay sobbing or shouting in promiscuous heaps. More than all, the negroes sang and screamed and prayed. Several, under the influence of what is technically called 'the jerks,' were plunging and pitching about with convulsive energy. The great object of all seemed to be, to see who could make the greatest noise. . . .

'Bless my poor soul!' screamed the preacher in the pulpit; 'ef yonder aint a squad in that corner that we aint got one outen yet! It'll never do'—raising his voice—'you must come outen that! Brother Fant, fetch up that youngster in the blue coat! I see the Lord's a-workin' upon him! Fetch him along—glory—yes!—hold to him!'

'Keep the thing warm!' roared a sensual seeming man, of stout mould and florid countenance, who was exhorting among a bevy of young women, upon whom he was lavishing caresses. 'Keep the thing warm, breethring!—come to the Lord, honey!' he added, as he vigorously hugged one of the damsels he sought to save. . . .

'Gl-O-*ree*!' yelled a huge, greasy negro woman, as in a fit of the jerks, she threw herself convulsively from her feet, and fell 'like a thousand of brick,' across a diminutive old man in a little round hat, who was speaking consolation to one of the mourners.

'Good Lord, have mercy!' ejaculated the little man earnestly and unaffectedly, as he strove to crawl from under the sable mass which was crushing him.

In another part of the square a dozen old women were singing. They were in a state of absolute ecstasy, as their shrill pipes gave forth. . . .

Near these last, stood a delicate woman in that hysterical condition in which the nerves are incontrollable and which is vulgarly—and almost blasphemously —termed the 'holy laugh.' A hideous grin distorted her mouth, and was accompanied by a maniac's chuckle; while every muscle and nerve of her face twitched and jerked in horrible spasms.[7]

For those who know the character Simon Suggs it is no surprise that his progress at this camp meeting is from hardened sinner to "heartfelt" penitent at the mourner's bench, and in due course to gloriously happy "regenerate" at the testimonial platform, holding forth with heated enthusiasm about the ecstasies of personal salvation. But the progress does not end there. Simon is considered the prime convert of the day. We find him taking charge of the meeting, and finally cantering off on his horse with the collection money in his pocket—a love offering from the group to the new church Simon promises to found.

It is essential in understanding the style of this mountebank to know the manner in which the money was secured, for the reverend Bela Bugg was himself fond of the collection plate and demanded that Suggs turn the money over to him. Simon's immediate reply was that the money had not been properly prayed over.

'You see that krick swamp?' asked Suggs—'I'm gwine down in *thar*, and I'm gwine to lay this money down so' . . . 'and I'm gwine to git on these here knees' . . . 'and I'm n-e-v-e-r gwine to quit the grit ontwell I feel it's got the blessin! And nobody aint got to be thar but me!'[8]

Captain Suggs "struck" for the swamp all right, but his horse was there before him already saddled.

To understand the frontier ethic implicit in humor such as this it is essential to be aware of the motto which was Simon's guiding principle. That motto was, "It's good to be shifty in a new country";[9] it expresses succinctly the attitude implicit in each of the sketches to be examined here. Traditionally the motto has been interpreted as expressing a permissive ethic in which success is the only criterion. However, in the light of Hooper's humorous but scathing description of the super-religiosity, the excessive naivete, hypocrisy, and grotesque emotionalism of the camp meeting scenes, it would seem that the reader would be relieved to find even a rascal such as Simon Suggs with sense enough to appraise the situation realistically. It would seem that we would be as delighted to see the shifty Simon abscond with the money as we are to see Brer Rabbit escape into the briar patch, or the third little pig escape from the wolf. Simon is a sympathetic rogue whose shiftiness should not be taken as a categorical endorsement of the principle of success by any means; rather it must be interpreted in terms of the kind of victims he chooses, the kind of craft he uses, and his attitude toward his success and failure. His victims are always ludicrous, his craft never entails malice, and his attitude toward success or failure is one of almost total disinterest. Simon, like Tom Sawyer, is more concerned about the stylistic excellence with which a hoax may be conducted, and Hooper, like Huck Finn, thinks of religious sentimentality and naiveté as "tears and flapdoodle." Viewed in its context, the "shiftiness" of Simon's motto is more an appeal for common sense than an endorsement of unbridled chicanery.

George Washington Harris's hero Sut Lovingood is another frontier prankster who found the camp meeting an appropriate setting for hoax and entertainment. Sut is more the thoroughgoing roughneck than Captain Suggs, and in addition he is not above such motives as personal revenge. In Harris's camp meeting sketch "Parson Bullen's Lizards"[10] we find Sut Lovingood taking his revenge upon one Parson Bullen for having told on him and a young lady named

Sally for engaging in an innocent conversation in a huckleberry thicket during a camp meeting at Rattlesnake Springs. In order to effect his revenge, Sut pretends conversion and sits at the preacher's feet during the sermon. There, and at the height of Parson Bullen's description of the torments of hell and the dreaded "Hell-serpents," Sut slips three lizards up the preacher's pants legs. The frantic activity of the preacher and the confusion and excitement of the crowd are drawn to extremes which reveal Harris at his descriptive best. The Parson finally throws off all his clothes and escapes to the woods. The revenge is recounted as complete and lasting in Sut's report of the event to the boys at Capehart's Doggery:

Ole Barebelly Bullen, as they calls him now, never preached again [until] yesterday, and he hadn't the first durned woman to hear him. . . . Parsons generally have a pow'ful strong hold on women, but, hoss, I tell you there ain't many of 'em kin run naked over and through a crowd of three hundred women and not injure their character some.[11]

Another camp meeting sketch emphasizing similarities of incident, technique, and attitude found in Old Southwest humor is the William C. Hall's story of "How Sally Hooter Got Snake-Bit."[12] The entire Hooter family packed up to attend this particular camp meeting. Among the food they took was a sausage described as being " 'bout as big as your arm, and long enuff to eat er week. . . ." Coincidental with the inclusion of this particular delicacy was a disagreement between Sally and her father, Mike Hooter, over the purchase of a bustle from a Yankee peddler. Mike had denied Sally the bustle, but when preaching time came he discovered that Sally had a "whoppin' big lump on behind," and that the sausage was missing. The meeting began, and the narrator's opening description of it will indicate something of the author's attitude toward camp meetings:

Brother James was loud that day! Thar he was, with the Bible on er board—stickin 'tween two saplins, and he was er cummin' down on it with his two fists worse nor maulin rails; and er stompin' his feet, an' er slobberin' at the mouth, an' er cuttin' up shines worse nor er bob'tail bull in fly time! . . . Torectly I spy the heatherns. They commence taken' on, and the spirit begin to move um for true—for brother Sturtevant's old nigger Cain, an' all uv um, they 'gin to kinder groan an' whine, an' reel erbout like er corn stalk in er

storm, an' Brother Grindle, he begin er rubbin' his hands an' slappin' um together, an' scramblin' about on his knees, an' er cuttin' up like mad! In about
a minit, I hearn the all firedest to do, down 'mongst the wimmin, that ever
cum along, an' when I kinder cast my eye over that way, I spy my Sal er
rarein' an' er pitchin', er rippin' an' er tarein' an er shoutin' like flinders![13]

Of course, everyone mistakes Sally's paroxysms as genuine manifestations of her conviction of sin, and many of the matrons nearby
offer their assistance by wrestling the poor girl to the ground. After
much confusion it is discovered that Sally's seizure had not been
precipitated by her sense of guilt, but by her fear of a snake. The
snake is found to be only the sausage she had used as a substitute
for the bustle her father had refused her; it had become untied and
had slipped down. This was the source of Sally's "religious" experience.

It seems significant that all these humorists found the camp meeting scene such an appropriate one on which to practice their art,
an art in which hoax and exaggeration play such an important part.
The Mike Hooter story, purported to be about a monstrous snake,
is, in part, an excuse for the storyteller to relate both the predica-
ment caused by Sally's pretensiousness and the exaggerated reactions of the brethren and sisters. The reader discovers Mike's story
to be about something other than it promised to be—"about how
Sally Hooter got snake-bit"; Sally's sausage is taken to be something it is not—a bustle; Sally takes her own sausage-bustle to be
something it is not—a snake; and the brethren take Sally's fright to
be something it is not—conversion. It seems legitimate for the reader
to associate this pattern of mistakenness with the delusiveness of
camp meeting religious experience.

Certainly these humorists found the camp meeting a natural setting for the presentation of boisterous comic incidents typical of
their humor, but their interest in the camp meeting does not seem
to end with its appropriateness as a comic setting. The humor is
not only funny, it is derisive of certain elements in frontier religion, and the common-sense ethic which runs through the humor
seems to caution the reader against an excessively emotional Beulah-
land religion. Such an appeal to common sense through humor appears repeatedly in American culture. It runs at least from Ben
Franklin to Mark Twain; it is as prevalent in children's stories as in

Union propaganda—the Uncle Remus warning, "You can't run away from trouble," expresses much the same attitude as Joe Hill's ironic labor song refrain, "You'll get pie in the sky when you die." In the camp meeting sketches of the Old Southwest we find this attitude of skeptical common sense, expressed against a background of emotional indulgence seldom found in the history of religion.

NOTES

1. William Warren Sweet, *Revivalism in America: Its Origin and Decline* (New York, 1944), p. 122.

2. Charles H. Johnson, *The Frontier Camp Meeting* (Dallas, 1955), p. 51.

3. James B. Finley, *Autobiography of the Reverend James B. Finley; or Pioneer Life in the West*, ed. W. P. Strickland (Cincinnati, 1853), pp. 166, 167.

4. Johnson, *The Frontier Camp Meeting*, p. 99.

5. *Porter's Spirit*, vol. I, no. 18 (Jan. 3, 1857), p. 288.

6. Johnson J. Hooper, "Simon Suggs Attends a Camp Meeting," in *Native American Humor*, ed. Walter Blair (San Francisco, 1960), pp. 316-325.

7. *Ibid.*, pp. 317, 318.

8. *Ibid.*, p. 325.

9. Blair, Introduction to *Native American Humor*, p. 86.

10. George Washington Harris, *Sut Lovingood*, ed. Brom Weber (New York, 1954), pp. 79-81.

11. *Ibid.*, p. 90.

12. In *Polly Peablossom's Wedding and Other Tales*, ed. T. A. Burke (Philadelphia, 1851), pp. 68-74.

13. *Ibid.*, pp. 71, 72.

Politics
In O. Henry's Stories

By E. HUDSON LONG

O. HENRY once wrote, "I was born and raised in 'No'th Ca'lina' and at eighteen went to Texas and ran wild on the prairies."[1]

At that time in North Carolina and Texas all minorities were spoken of disparagingly; it was a part of our folk custom. O. Henry inherited this attitude and never outgrew it. Today some of his racial humor seems appalling, but in other respects he was our contemporary. And his inherited attitudes never led to bigotry against individuals. In "The Guardian of the Accolade" the old Negro, Uncle Bushrod, had served the Weymouth family so faithfully that he carried a key to the vault of the Weymouth bank. "The Emancipation of Billy" presents another Negro, Thomas Jefferson Pemberton, who was regarded as a "member of de fambly" (p. 473).[2] And in "A Municipal Report" Caesar, the old hack driver, shoulders the responsibility of protecting the last member of the impoverished Adair family from her brutal Southern husband, proudly saying, "She has reso'ces, suh; she has reso'ces" (p. 1561). As Leonidas W. Payne, Jr., of the University of Texas wrote of O. Henry, "He loved truth and justice and fair play, and he respected true manhood and womanhood wherever he found it. He was infatuated with common humanity. He was the truest democrat of all."[3]

This liberal attitude was expressed in *The Rolling Stone* for May 12, 1894:

General Coxey has made a great blunder. He and his fellows should have gone to Washington clad in broadcloth and fine garments, and backed by a big bank roll, as the iron, steel, sugar, and other lobbying delegations do. He should have taken apartments at the Arlington, and given receptions and dinners. That's the way to get legislation at the hands of the American congress.

This thing of leading a few half clothed and worse fed working men to the capitol grounds to indulge in the vulgar and old-fashioned peaceable assemblage to petition for redress of grievances, with not a dollar of boodle in sight for the oppressed and overworked members of congress, was of course an outrage, and so the perpetrators were promptly squelched by the strong hand of the "law."

Earlier in a letter back home from the Dull Ranch young Porter, following the tradition of our native folk humorists, wrote that a fellow North Carolinian, Ed Brockman, "Wears a red sash and swears so fluently that he has been mistaken often for a member of the Texas Legislature."[4]

In Austin O. Henry approved of the political appointments: "If other grounds were less abundant, Texas should be well up in the lists of glory as the grateful republic. For both as republic and state, it has busily heaped honors and solid rewards upon its sons who rescued it from the wilderness" (p. 488). However, in the tradition of our folk humor, he continued to poke fun at the legislature.

A Texas ranchman, Bud Oakley in "Law and Order," complained, "Them legislators set up there at Austin and don't do nothing but make laws against kerosene oil and schoolbooks being brought into the state. I reckon they was afraid some man would go home some evening after work and light up and get an education and go to work and make laws to repeal aforesaid laws" (p. 915).

"Art and the Bronco" deals also with the Texas legislature. Senator Mullens of the San Saba country wished to have a picture of a stampeding steer purchased by the state, while Senator Kinney needed support for an irrigation bill he was sponsoring. A *quid pro quo* was soon arranged. "Senators Kinney and Mullens came to an understanding in the matter of irrigation and art while partaking of long drinks in the cafe of the Empire Hotel" (p. 402).

In "The Marquis and Miss Sally" O. Henry, who was always interested in the folk customs of the range, has described a candidate for reelection to the legislature visiting the Diamond-Cross ranch, where the cowboys pretend that his high silk hat is some deadly varmint and shoot it full of holes. The unhappy candidate, mindful of the sixty votes on the ranch, goes along with the horseplay, thanking the boys for saving his life.

While in Honduras O. Henry became intrigued with the political chicanery, and he later involved his characters in such plots. Denver Galloway dispensed money on an election until it was like "a Bryan barbecue in Texas" (p. 509). Denver, who had managed the banner district in New York, thought the same methods would work elsewhere for his Latin candidate: "He needs a campaign manager to go down and whoop things up for him—to get the boys in line and the new two-dollar bills afloat and the babies kissed and the machine in running order" (p. 511). But when his friend Sully tried to tell him things were different and he would have no more effect than "a Congressman from North Dakota trying to get an appropriation for a lighthouse and a coast survey," Denver enthusiastically replied, "We get the heelers out with the crackly two-spots, and coal tickets, and orders for groceries, and have a couple of picnics out under the banyan trees, and dances in the Firemen's Hall—and the usual things. But first of all, Sully, I'm going to have the biggest clam-bake down on the beach that was ever seen south of the tropic of Capricorn" (pp. 513-514). Told that no clams existed in the country and learning what the general fare of the natives consisted of, Denver exploded that a man who would eat such stuff "ought to have his vote challenged" (p. 514).

During his stay in Honduras O. Henry noted that Americans sometimes had to appeal to the British consul for protection. In "The Phonograph and the Graft" the United States consul admits, "Twice before, I have cabled our government for a couple of gunboats to protect American citizens. The first time the Department sent me a pair of gum boots. The other time was when a man named Pease was going to be executed here. They referred that appeal to the Secretary of Agriculture" (p. 590). Barnard O'Keefe, about to be shot in a Central American prison, despite his loyal political support of "the Great Father in Washington" had found his case ignored:

" . . . the United States of America had overruled his appeal for protection, and had instructed Private Secretary Cortelyou to reduce his estimate of the Republican majority for 1905 by one vote" (p. 536).

The story "The Fourth in Salvador" tells how a group of Americans celebrating Independence Day accidentally contributed to the success of a revolution; whereupon Billy Casparis, who had forfeited $1,000 to the deposed government for failure to keep his contract to manufacture ice, had his money returned by the new one, and instead of making ice was allowed to display a chunk of molded glass as a substitute.

For fifteen years Judson Tate in another Latin country was the "ruling power behind old Sancho Benavides, the Royal High Thumbscrew of the republic" (p. 391). Benavides, the Liberator, would hold office for a few terms, then appoint his successor for a while until he decided to return. "He'd have been sure called the Roosevelt of the Southern Continent," says O. Henry, "if it hadn't been that Grover Cleveland was President at the time" (p. 391). Bud Kingsbury, a Texan on his first trip to New York, was rattled until he said to himself, "Here, now, Bud; they're just plain folks like you and Geronimo and Grover Cleveland and the Watson boys . . ." (p. 844).

Describing Patrick Shane in "Supply and Demand," O. Henry says, "I've seen United States Senators of his style of features and build, also head-waiters and cops" (p. 726). Shane, who had set himself up in South America as head of a tribe of Indians who brought gold to him, called himself the "Big Stick," a reference to Roosevelt. Later there is a reference to the silver standard, advocated by William Jennings Bryan and Tom Watson, Bryan's running mate in 1896. Finch, who sought to share Shane's racket with the Indians, says, "Talk to 'em like a born anti-Bryanite. . . . Remind 'em that Tom Watson's gone back to Georgia" (p. 730).

William Jennings Bryan, though thrice defeated in attempts to become president, was the leader of the Democratic party for thirty years and had a loyal following, of which O. Henry took note when he has a character say in "Shearing the Wolf," ". . . we might as well have tried to keep the man who rolls peanuts with a toothpick from betting on Bryan's election" (p. 302). In "A Night in New

Arabia" the grocer's young man was promised a twenty-dollar raise at Christmas "if Bryan couldn't think of any harder name to call a Republican than a 'postponer' " (p. 1589).

Long before the Hoovercrats, Dixiecrats, and Democrats for Eisenhower, there was the dissident who called himself "Roosevelt-Democrat"(p. 762). O. Henry has also included him. In "The Call of the Tame" the popular leader is called "King Teddy" (p. 1529). And Theodore Roosevelt's methods of securing the Panama Canal are briefly mentioned, "You know that was about the time they staged them property revolutions down there, that wound up in the fifth act with the thrilling canal scene where Uncle Sam has nine curtain-calls holding Miss Panama by the hand, while the blood-hounds keep Senator Morgan treed up in a cocoanut-palm" (p. 539). Senator John Tyler Morgan of Alabama was a leading advocate of the canal but strongly favored constructing it across Nicaragua instead of Panama.

Though Colonel Telfair, editor of *The Rose of Dixie* in the story by that name, generally confined his interest to the South, he did run a picture of "Fighting Bob" LaFollette of Wisconsin, who advocated a just tariff to protect agriculture, tax reform, and government supervision of all public utilities. And he did print a speech by Teddy Roosevelt because he was kin to the Bulloch family of Georgia (p. 689).

Chauncey Depew of the New York Central Railroad, who had joined with "Boss" Platt in backing Roosevelt for governor of New York to hide a party record of graft and corruption, drew O. Henry's interest. Describing a Latin American dictator, O. Henry wrote, "He's a kind of combination of Julius Caesar, Lucifer and Chauncey Depew done in sepia" (p. 651).

A flamboyant figure from Texas was Senator Joseph Weldon Bailey. In "The Moment of Victory" O. Henry wrote, "The next day the battleship *Maine* was blown up, and then pretty soon somebody—I reckon it was Joe Bailey or Ben Tillman, or maybe the Government—declared war against Spain" (p. 757). Once when Senator Bailey was speaking in Texas a man lately arrived at the gathering asked an old Negro on the edge of the crowd to identify the speaker for him, to which the old man replied, "I ain't cotch his name, but he cert'nly do recommen' his self mos' high." The

Tillman alluded to was an uneducated son of the soil who appealed to the "patched breeches and one gallus" vote in South Carolina, a different sort from the flowery Bailey.

Ben Granger of the story, whose attitude toward the Spanish-American War finds its sympathetic counterpart today with regard to Viet Nam, stated, "I want to go back home. I don't care whether Cuba sinks or swims, and I don't give a pipeful of rabbit tobacco whether Queen Sophia Christina or Charlie Culberson rules these fairy isles; and I don't want my name on any list except the list of survivors" (p. 760). Senator Charles A. Culberson represented Texas from 1899 to 1923. O. Henry's attitude to the war in general was fully expressed through Ben Granger: "It seemed like a waste of life to me. I was at Coney Island when I went to New York once, and one of them down-hill skidding apparatuses they call 'roller coasters' flew the track and killed a man in a brown sack-suit. Whenever the Spaniards shot one of our men, it struck me as just about as unnecessary and regrettable as that was" (p. 758).

O. Henry was aware of imperialistic exploitation. "For there are yet tales of the Spanish Main," he wrote. "Taken and retaken by sea rovers, by adverse powers and by sudden uprisings of rebellious factions, the historic 300 miles of adventurous coast has scarcely known for hundreds of years whom rightly to call its master. . . . The hucksters of Germany, France, and Sicily now bag its small change across their counters" (pp. 553-554).

A Democrat by inheritance, O. Henry was also one through his progressive ideas and his zeal for reform. In "The Moment of Victory" he has Ben Granger state, "Our company was among the first to land in Cuba and strike terror into the hearts of the foe. I'm not going to give you a history of the war; I'm just dragging it in to fill out my story about Willie Robbins, just as the Republican party dragged it in to help out the election in 1898" (p. 757). O. Henry also refers to a character as "being of sound body but a Republican mind" (p. 542).

In "Squaring the Circle" O. Henry states that a "Republican Missouri" would be a "rather curious product" (p. 1309). And Jeff Peters, speaking of seeds of self-destruction, refers to "a rooster that crows near a Georgia colored Methodist camp meeting, or a Republican announcing himself a candidate for governor of Texas"

(p. 267). In a burlesque, "Tracked to Doom," a character complains, "Bah! those Democrats. They have ruined the country. With their income tax and their free trade, they have destroyed the millionaire business" (p. 1022).

With his story "Tictocq" O. Henry presents a burlesque of a well-known Populist candidate from Kansas known as "Sockless Jerry" Simpson, who accused by his opponents of wearing socks, pleaded, "I swear before heaven that I never wore a pair of socks in my life. It is all a devilish campaign lie" (p. 1020). Tictocq, O. Henry's farcical French detective, had come to Austin to investigate "a treaty between the Emperor Charlemagne and Governor Roberts, which expressly provides for the north gate of the Capital grounds being kept open" (p. 1015). Governor Oran M. Roberts, whose supporters wanted him for a third term, had been prominent for decades in Texas politics and was known as the "Old Alcalde."

In "A Snapshot at the President" O. Henry imagines Grover Cleveland conversing with Tom Ochiltree, who had been a major in Hood's Brigade and a member of Congress from the Galveston district. President Cleveland then refers to Senator Roger Q. Mills of Texas, who strongly advocated tariff reform: "I think the greatest two speeches I ever heard were his address before the Senate advocating the removal of the tariff on salt and increasing it on the chloride of sodium" (p. 1029).

At times O. Henry joshed his own party. In an era of Republican ascendancy Johnny Atwood, a Democrat, was appointed consul at Coralio because, O. Henry says, "Among other accidents of that year was a Democratic president" (p. 585). Johnny lounged in a hammock that had become his "official reclining place" saying, "You can't expect a Democrat to work during his first term of holding office" (p. 586).

When Jeff Peters and Andy Tucker undertake to secure a political appointment for their friend Bill Humble, Jeff says, "Now Andy, for the first time in our lives we've got to do a real dishonest act." Their first thought is to "hand over $500 . . . to the chairman of the national campaign committee, get a receipt, lay the receipt on the President's desk and tell him about Bill" (p. 289). However, they soon find themselves in the hands of a lobbyist.

O. Henry's irony about politics also included Wall Street. "Holding Up a Train" was derived from material furnished him by the outlaw Al Jennings, who declared that the train robber's greatest fear was being betrayed for a reward. To which O. Henry added, "And it is one of the reasons why the train-robbing profession is not so pleasant a one as either of its collateral branches—politics or cornering the market" (p. 839).

O. Henry's character Andy Tucker once questions his friend Jeff Peters about different forms of graft. Jeff replies, "There are two kinds of grafts that ought to be wiped out by law. I mean Wall Street speculation and burglary." Andy assents, "Nearly everybody will agree with you as to one of them." To which Jeff replies, "Well, burglary ought to be wiped out, too" (p. 315).

In New York O. Henry saw the grime and squalor of the slums. He knew the underworld and the leaders who controlled the lesser criminals. He was aware of the political connections between crime and those who were supposed to enforce the laws, which unfortunately has become a part of the folklore of politics.

Dempsey Donovan in "The Coming-Out of Maggie" was never "troubled by trouble." As one of "Big Mike" O'Sullivan's lieutenants, "No cop dared to arrest him." If he broke someone's head or shot somebody the worst that could happen was to receive a message, "The Cap'n'd like to see ye a few minutes round to the office whin ye have time, Dempsey, me boy" (p. 31).

"Roses, Ruses and Romance" mentions the "story of a political boss who won the love of a Fifth Avenue belle by blacking her eye and refusing to vote for an iniquitous ordinance (it doesn't say whether it was in the Street Cleaning Department or Congress)" (p. 1312). Billy McMahan in "The Social Triangle" was the political leader of his district. "Upon him the Tiger purred, and his hand held manna to scatter" (p. 1420). "Past One at Rooney's" tells of Cork McManus, unfortunately involved with the police while his district leader was visiting Europe. "Until Tim Corrigan should return from his jaunt among Kings and Princes and hold up his big white finger in private offices, it was unsafe for Cork in any of the old haunts of his gang" (p. 1606). In "A Sacrifice Hit" O. Henry refers to dishonesty in New York state government as "Albany grabs" (p. 1153).

He once told Mabel Wagnalls, "No one who has not known it can imagine the misery of poverty," earnestly adding, "Poverty is so terrible and so common, we should all do more than we do—much more—to relieve it."[5] Actually O. Henry put his theories into practice. It was his custom to mingle with the derelicts along the Bowery or waterfront and the paupers drifting through the parks or standing in lines to get a bed. Always he gave them money. Once with a friend he handed a beggar a twenty-dollar gold piece. When the man, who was grateful and felt that O. Henry had mistaken the gold piece for another coin, hurried after them, O. Henry, chagrined that his generosity had been exposed, brusquely told the man to go along. He never wanted his charities to be known, and was "mortified that his friend should have detected his ruse."[6]

O. Henry mingled with the indigents in Union Square and Madison Square, giving them handouts and listening to the tales of those unfortunates cast aside by the city's currents. In "The Fifth Wheel" we see the destitute forming into the bed line, unfortunates at whose stories of lost position through illness or other misfortunes "the city yawns at every day" (p. 66). His preference for democracy is emphatic in the preface to *The Four Million*:

Not very long ago someone invented the assertion that there were only "Four Hundred" people in New York City who were really worth noticing. But a wiser man has arisen—the census taker—and his larger estimate of human interest has been preferred in marking out the field of these little stories of the "Four Million."

O. Henry's character Alexander Blinker was infused with the same Jeffersonian Democracy as his creator. On a trip to Coney Island, "He no longer saw a mass of vulgarians seeking gross joys. He now looked clearly upon a hundred thousand true idealists" (p. 1407). And with the spirit that animated the sage of Monticello, "He no longer saw a rabble, but his brothers seeking the ideal" (p. 1408).

Long before there was any idea of the "Great Society" O. Henry spoke strongly for slum clearance and the alleviation of those cruelly trapped there. With "The Guilty Party" and "Brickdust Row" he depicted the degrading effect on the victims, while the ruthless owners of the slums amassed fortunes at their expense. A character in "Rus in Urbe," dining on a cool roof garden during a hot August night, says to his callous friend, " . . . you might think about the kids down in Delancey and Hester streets lying out on the fire-escapes with their tongues hanging out, trying to get a breath of air that hasn't been fried on both sides" (p. 798).

O. Henry saw the need to force unscrupulous employers, who with no moral conscience, unrestrained greed, and utter contempt for human rights, worked their employees at bare-subsistence wages. With "The Skylight Room," "The Third Ingredient," and "An Unfinished Story" he depicted the plight of such employees. In the latter story he dipped his pen in acid to describe the hardships of Dulcie deprived of "those joys that belong to woman by virtue of all the unwritten, sacred, natural, inactive ordinances of the equity of heaven" (p. 74). So effective were O. Henry's stories about the abuses of the helpless that Theodore Roosevelt stated, "It was O. Henry who started me on my campaign for the office girls."[7]

O. Henry blended realism and romance to focus the reader's attention on his everyday material through which the less fortunate are revealed in their daily struggle for existence, often drab or sunken, but seldom without hope. He had a double purpose, which was to write stories that would sell and at the same time speak strongly for reform. The S. S. McClure syndicate with its emphasis on muckraking provided a ready market, and O. Henry was naturally in sympathy with Theodore Roosevelt's "trust busting" and his attacks on "malefactors of great wealth." With a keen understanding of the problems of the underprivileged and a belief in man's ability to better his position if given a chance, he satisfied his readers with humor, sensation, and sentiment while seriously developing his social themes in the tradition of our folk humorists.

NOTES

1.   C. Alphonso Smith, *O. Henry Biography* (Doubleday, Page & Company, 1916), p. 46.

2.   The page numbers after each quotation from O. Henry refer to *Complete Works of O. Henry* (2 vols.; Garden City, N. Y.: Doubleday & Co., 1953).

3.   "The Humor of O. Henry," *Texas Review*, IV (October 1918), 36.

4.   E. Hudson Long, *O. Henry: The Man and His Work* (Philadelphia: University of Pennsylvania Press, 1949), p. 37.

5.   *Letters to Lithopolis* (Garden City, N. Y.: Doubleday, Page & Company, 1922), p. xxiv.

6.   "Anecdotes of O. Henry," *Mentor*, XI (Feb. 1923), 45.

7.   *Ibid.*, p. d (page so numbered).

Myth In
The Winter Of Our Discontent

By KYRA JONES

IN his last novel,
The Winter of Our Discontent, John Steinbeck drastically altered
his usual mythological content. In this novel he reversed the structural functions which he habitually assigned to myth and reality.
Again and again he had written about groups of people living in
some kind of enclave apart from the outside world. They are in a
kind of mythological state, an earthly paradise; whenever reality
tries to intrude upon them and so move them into a profane
state, they repel the intrusions and the intruders threatening their
mode of existence. Thus myth vanquishes reality in the plot. In
The Winter of Our Discontent reality is the victor. The movement
is away from the mythic and toward profane reality; this is the
source and nature of the tragedy in *The Winter of Our Discontent*.
Ethan Allen Hawley, under pressure from his family and society to
seek wealth and status, commits two crimes of betrayal which he
cannot rectify. In the end he passes a severe moral judgment upon
himself and reaches the point of suicide, but he performs no act of
expiation and achieves no redemption. By showing, negatively in
this novel, what happens when the profane triumphs over the sacred,

Steinbeck reemphasized the high valuation which he had always placed upon living mythologically.

The distinction between the sacred and the profane which I have just made use of has gained currency through the writings of Mircea Eliade.[1] Beginning with the most ancient experience of man, Eliade identifies the chief component of the sacred as some manifestation of the divine, the more than human. The profane lacks this component. Eliade applies his distinction to time and place and thus separates myth and reality; sacred time and place belong to myth and profane time and place belong to reality. Primitive or archaic people believe that sacred time can be renewed or restored by performing rituals and reciting myths. Any place can be sacralized in the same way. Profane time and place cannot be so evoked or restored. For primitives the real is the sacred, so that for them reality is equivalent to the mythic. Moderns think of the mythic as opposite and contradictory to the real. And they recognize only time that is irreversible and place that is fixed, as in secular history.

An understanding of the mythological pattern common to Steinbeck's earlier works is prerequisite to an analysis of myth in *The Winter of Our Discontent*. Steinbeck's mythological expression is essentially in harmony with the archaic view of life which allows for the re-creation of the cosmos and for the reality of a paradisal existence achieved through recitation of myth and enactment of ritual. In his early novels, this quest for an archaic type of reality involves living in or finding the proper ("sacred") place, as it did in primitive times. It involves a movement of the protagonists from one area to another and/or an actual conflict between the "primitive" and the "civilized" elements of society.

Steinbeck's early works are dominated by four essential characteristics of archaic mythology: the exploration and/or settlement of an unfamiliar territory, an act repetitive of the creation of the universe; the sacrality of the family unit and/or the group or community of fellows; the lack of stress on or interest in the autonomy of the individual and the complexities of the particular psyche; and the abundance of archetypal rituals and figures.[2] But the conflict between this sacred mode of existence and the profane world of modern civilization is a necessary counterpart to these essentials. Almost invariably, the protagonists of the early novels are primitives, characterized by poverty, association with the land, tribal unity, ancestor worship, alien attributes, et cetera, and engaged in sacred quest, flight from and/or combat with civilized society. The plot structures are generally based upon this struggle, while the characterization is archetypal.

Reality with a small "r," the thematic opposite of Steinbeckian myth, is usually represented as a force or a system, at worst threatening the primitives as in *To a God Unknown*, *The Grapes of Wrath*, *The Pearl*, and *In Dubious Battle*, and at best physically surrounding them as in *The Red Pony*, *Cannery Row*, *Sweet Thursday*, *East of Eden*, and *The Wayward Bus*. In the early Steinbeck, modern society or "the profane" performs a mythical role in an essentially mythic structure, a subordinate role of creative opposition.

For Steinbeck, as for the primitive, myth is "Reality," with a capital "R." In other words, the only "Real" existence is one that is archaically ordained, an existence defined by cosmic participation and responsibility. Conventional reality is the condition of modern civilization in which values are individual, material, and temporal. In *The Winter of Our Discontent*, Steinbeck reverses the structural roles which he usually assigns to myth and reality, radically changing his mode of expression in order to give new emphasis to his oft-repeated theme. He enters the world of modern society, giving emphasis to ordinary reality while reducing his usual mythological content to fantasy. The role of archaic myth is confined to that of the pangs of an inflamed, evolutionary appendix, and religious myth is limited to Judeo-Christian parallels. The latter is the only myth integral to the novel, and it serves to anchor irrevocably the situation in profane time. In this manner, Steinbeck outlines the incidental role of myth in modern life and the consequences of such a subjugation of man's primal heritage and impulse.

Mircea Eliade, my authority on archaic myth, states that the fall of man was a fall into history and that history constitutes the profane time of duration. It can be argued that the concept of time implicit in the Old Testament is more reminiscent of the timelessness of primitive religion than of the historical time of the New Testament; but Steinbeck, in *The Winter of Our Discontent*, takes no account of this argument. For Steinbeck, Adam's loss is irrevocable. Unless the Steinbeckian Adam-figure has a parallel mythological identification with Christ and the archaic savior/hero, e.g., Joseph Wayne of *To a God Unknown*, his mythical identity is restricted by the author to that of fallen man. In *The Winter of Our Discontent*, Steinbeck makes this point clear. He creates Ethan, a protagonist who unites the Old and New Testament figures of Adam, Cain, and Judas in the person of modern man.

The story, even stripped of metaphor and symbol, cannot be extracted from the myth of the fall. The protagonist is Ethan Allen Hawley, a descendant of one of the original settlers of Old Baytown. Prompted by the contrived fortunetelling of the prostitute, Ethan's wife Mary goads him into accepting the temptation of wealth. Possessed of and by the knowledge of good and evil, this man plunges himself into modern society and its ethics. He betrays his employer Marullo, destroys his friend Danny, and gains the world. He and his wife Mary bicker, and his children hate each other. All the while, Ethan looks to the future for the redemption of his purity. Even in his desolation at the end of the novel, he hopes for mortality and immortality in and through his daughter Ellen. Ethan is an Adam-figure; Mary is Eve; and their children are the children of Adam.

Character parallels to other figures of the Old and New Testaments reinforce the all-pervasive fallen-man theme, for they are confined to the Judas and Genesis myths. Danny Taylor and Marullo, both alien members of the community, figure centrally in this supportive mythology. It is Ethan's betrayal of these two men, his friend and his employer, which extends his characterization from the simple Adam-figure to that of Cain and Judas.

Multilayered Biblical parallels of this sort are not in the least unusual in Steinbeck. A comparison of these in *The Winter of Our Discontent* with those in the earlier novels will, however, reveal an elemental difference between the two—the absence of a god or savior figure. In the early novels, this symbolic figure is firmly and directly rooted in archaic myth. Biblical parallels embrace both Eastern and primitive religion and rites. The God or the Christ is also the fecundator, chieftain, sometimes a shaman, and, most importantly, the creator and perpetuator of a way of life.

The lack of a mythical god or savior figure in *The Winter of Our Discontent* is emphasized by the ironic characterization of Mr.

Baker, the president of the bank. He personifies the sterility of modern time, religion, and materialism; yet he functions as the archaic patriarch-deity of the earlier novels. By virtue of his position at the bank, Mr. Baker is the leading citizen of New Baytown and he takes his responsibility most seriously. He perpetuates the puritanism and self-rightous piracy of the way of life ordained by his ancestors, who were among the first to inhabit this new world. Likewise, he dictates and performs the rituals, public and private, of the community. His ceremony of opening the bank vault is repeatedly described in religious imagery; it signals the advent of day. Mr. Baker receives the members of his community in a ritual and formal manner. He sits in his large chair, which is elevated and placed behind an altar-like desk. His communicants approach as penitents and/or supplicants. Both oracle and clairvoyant, Mr. Baker is served by an acolyte who names him "God Almighty."[3] Natural imagery, such as that in *To a God Unknown*, also supports the deification of this profane character. In this way Steinbeck applies the attributes, both in image and act, of an archaic atmospheric diety to the most profane embodiment of modern civilization.

Mr. Baker, the only god-figure of *The Winter of Our Discontent*, represents the money-worshiping religion of fallen man. His commandments are money, history, and progress. Far from being a fecundator, he is sterile and is the only man refused access to the village prostitute. His re-creation of the world involves the public shame of his long-time associates and friends, a secret gift of whiskey to the alcoholic Danny, and the compromise of the honest cop in town. A *deus otiosus* in reverse, he precipitates disaster and chaos, and then disappears. In this anomalous manner, Mr. Baker serves as the most obvious key to the inverted role of myth and reality in *The Winter of Our Discontent*.

The nature and use of the archaic myth *per se* in *The Winter of Our Discontent* is a more subtle indication of the changed role of reality and myth. In general, the nature of the archaic myth is nocturnal, vestigial in an evolutionary sense, and rationalized.

Archaic myth performs a role in *The Winter of Our Discontent* similar to that of modern civilization in Steinbeck's earlier novels. It serves both as contrast and as threat to the order of the community. Traditionally in Steinbeck, this role has been ascribed to the profane forces of civilization—witness *The Pearl*, *The Grapes of Wrath*, *East of Eden*, *The Pastures of Heaven*, *Pippin IV*.

Only two of the preceding novels, *Cup of Gold* and *In Dubious Battle*, exhibit a construct similar to that of *The Winter of Our Discontent*. In both of these archaic myth and ritual are misused by the protagonists in a manner similar to Ethan's pouring of the ancestral wine to consecrate his fall.

The ramifications of the nocturnal aspect of myth are manifold. Most of the archaic hierophanies occur at night, in night wanderings, or in darkness of one kind or another. And, night obviously implies the mythos of the moon with its mystique of death and fertility. To Steinbeck, lunar mythology is predominantly funereal. All of his obviously lunar characters are doomed to self-destruction of one form or another, e.g., Willie and Benjy in *To a God Unknown*, Henry Morgan in *Cup of Gold*, Tom Hamilton in *East of Eden*, and Tularecito in *The Pastures of Heaven*. Also, the Steinbeckian moon mythos frequently implies a feminine dominance, which according to Steinbeck is an unhealthy arrangement, as he illustrates in the moon imagery in *Cup of Gold* and more superbly in his short story "The Murder." Similarly, the waters of the sea, which exist under the domain of the moon both in myth and in *The Winter of Our Discontent*, are not imbued by Steinbeck with much of their ancient creative powers.

In this novel water lacks its traditional regenerative power. Most of the water images are of destruction and/or stagnation. Ritual baths, such as Ethan's shower after his betrayal of Danny and his attempted drowning, occur only as temporary purges and do not promise or even imply rebirth or regeneration. In *The Winter of Our Discontent*, Steinbeck does allow the moon and her mythological subjects a limited creative force; but the manifestations of this force do not exceed the level of those of the tidepool's spawning. The dark of night, of deep water, and of the prehuman stage in evolution (the tidepool) are equated metaphorically with the darkness of Ethan's subconscious mind. And, at the end of the novel, darkness is given a negative value in the ethical symbolism.

The two most pure evidences of archaic mythology in the novel, the cave and the talisman, are both subject to the mythos of the moon. To begin with, the cave is approached only at night. It is a cavity in the seawall of the Old Harbor, which occasionally is made inaccessible by the waters of the moon-governed tide. In Steinbeck's earlier novels, caves are not associated in any way with lunar mythology. Also, they are inland and naturally formed, and they appear as sites of healing, revelation, and rebirth.

At first glance, the cave in *The Winter of Our Discontent* exhibits archaically ordained functions and properties. It is the scene of Ethan's rites of passage. He has gone there the night before becoming a man in joining the service, before becoming a husband, and before becoming a father. There also he goes to communicate with his ancestors, escape the pressures of modern life, and attempt suicide. Nonetheless, the ambivalence of the lunar mythology also characterizes Ethan's relationship to the cave. It is there that he celebrates another rite of passage, that of his fall into modern society.

The talisman, brought from the Orient by some unidentified ancestor, is given an anomalous mythical construct similar to that of the cave. It is a round stone of undetermined composition, a kind of mound four inches in diameter. It feels like flesh and is always warm. When Ethan was very young it seemed to be a human breast, and then when he was a boy it became a yoni, a symbol of feminine sexuality. An unending, interweaving carved design went around it like a serpent without beginning or end; this feature puts it into the realm of the timeless and sacred. Like the cave, it is dominated by the mythos of the moon. For the most part, this talisman is approached in darkness; and only at night does it exert its powers over Ellen. Its changing colors derive from the phases of the moon as described in Steinbeck's short story "The Murder." Ethan's discovery of the talisman hidden in his pocket by Ellen prompts him to fight his way out of the cave, where he had intended to drown himself. As he holds it in his hand it gathers all the light in the cave and seems to be dark red—the color of blood. Ethan, the talisman, and Ellen are connected through light imagery; he knows that his light is forever extinguished, but he must return the light-collecting talisman to Ellen, the lightbearer, so that her own light will continue. This escape from the rising waters cannot be construed as Ethan's triumph over the sterility of Steinbeck's moon mythology, because it is prompted by the two entities mythically governed by the moon—the talisman and the daughter. Only once has this sacred stone braved the light of day. Ethan took it with him as a good-luck piece to insure the success of his bank robbery. At the last moment it became impossible and unnecessary for him to rob the bank—this was the good luck that it ironically brought.

Ethan's ancestor worship, evoked by the cave, talisman, and night thoughts, is also qualified by the profane. Ethan reveres his Aunt Deborah and his grandfather, the old Cap'n. His aunt, whose name means Judge of Israel, conducted his spiritual training. She taught him the Scriptures and much else besides. He thinks of her as a sibyl and pythoness who could recite magical and nonsensical words which he later remembered. He quotes two sentences in Old English, which he leaves untranslated and unexplained.[4] One is from Caedmon's *Genesis*: "The evil serpent deceived me with fair words." The other is from Alfred's translation of Boethius' *Consolation of Philosophy*: "If the lioness tastes blood she will bite her keeper first." These were indeed prophetic for Ethan, who succumbed to temptation and in carrying out his evil plan caused his friend Danny to die. Old Cap'n used to tell Ethan about the old days of whaling and sailing to the Orient, from which some ancestor had brought the talisman. He explained the tradition of "piracy" in the family as going back to the time when a Hawley was a privateer licensed to prey upon enemy ships upon the high seas. Aunt Deborah and old Cap'n together represent the Puritans and the pirates of Ethan's ancestry; and Ethan himself helpfully explains this phenomenon of his heritage. He insists, "Where they merged, they produced a hard-bitten, surviving bunch of monkeys."[5] On the other hand, Ethan abuses the memory of his gentle, scholarly father. Resentful of his father's loss of the family monies, Ethan scorns him, referring to him as "the fool."[6]

Even the initiatory rite, a most significant aspect of primitive religion, is given an ironic application in *The Winter of Our Discontent*. Ethan is reborn. All the imagery of initiation and its consequent rebirth are repeatedly evoked. However, in *The Winter of Our Discontent*, the new man and the new world are created and sustained in the mind of a single person; and the result is not the re-creation of an actual paradise. It is instead the moral disintegration of an individual, a fall into the profane. Steinbeck has given us precedents for the ironic use of the initiation and rebirth motif in

Henry Morgan of *Cup of Gold*, Jim Nolan of *In Dubious Battle*, and Adam Trask in *East of Eden*.

In addition to deliberately allowing the characters of *The Winter of Our Discontent* to misinterpret, misuse, and misappropriate archaic rites, Steinbeck employs yet another means of relegating primitive myth to a vestigial capacity. He allows Ethan to submit it to his quasi-rational analysis. Subjecting all events to analysis, Ethan rationalizes them out of any mythical existence: he wonders if fortunetelling might merely be a "psychic excercise"[7]; he decides that his relationship to his "Place" is not really a return-to-the-womb fixation;[8] and he considers that the mysteries of Ellen's sleepwalking might just be "children of my mind."[9] His position as narrator assures that nothing escapes Ethan's mental gymnastics.

The foreword of *The Winter of Our Discontent* immediately reveals that the book has a didactic purpose. Steinbeck admonishes: "Readers seeking to identify the fictional people and places here described would do better to inspect their own communities and search their own hearts, for this book is about a large part of America today." And what it is all about is a loss of the "Real" in the archaic sense and a substitution of the "real" in the modern sense. Even the vestiges of archaic sacrality are falsified by misuse and misinterpretation. At the beginning of the novel, Ethan accepts the false values of modern society and begins to pursue them; in the course of events he betrays Marullo and Danny and thus reaches the point of attaining wealth and status. The discovery that his son has cheated on a national contest to gain similar goals brings home to Ethan his own wrongdoing. He goes to the Place to commit suicide, but when he finds the talisman in his pocket, put there by his daughter, he knows that he must take it back to her so that her light will not go out as his has. Ethan will return from his symbolic death, but it is emphasized that his light has been extinguished forever. He cannot undo what he has done. Rejection of his now-assured fortune and position would not absolve him of his crime against Marullo, who has been deported, and Danny, who is dead. One can only assume that, at best, Ethan will lead an outwardly righteous and upright life—now that he is "King of the Mountain." [10]

It is Steinbeck's hope for change in effectiveness that apparently prompted his reversal of roles in his last novel. He had repeatedly dealt with both the sacred and the profane that he had witnessed in life; but he had done so with emphasis on characters who chose to live in accord with archaic, mythological values. Because he was not heard and understood, he changed his emphasis in *The Winter of Our Discontent* and concentrated on the "real" with a little "r." He turned away from his favored primitives and innocents to Ethan Allen Hawley, who knows and understands the meaning of the Real—the sacred and mythic—but nevertheless becomes a deliberate betrayer. Ethan suffers along with Christ during Holy Week, but he chooses and enacts the role of Judas. He is clearly shown to be in pursuit of false, profane values. Steinbeck was giving warning to modern America.

According to Steinbeck, the quest is to find one's relationship to the whole world; the pitfalls are moralism, materialism, and hypocrisy; and the archaic view of life is the most cosmic and therefore the most satisfactory—the most Real.

NOTES

1. See especially *The Myth of the Eternal Return*, trans. Willard R. Trask (New York: Pantheon Books, 1954); *Patterns in Comparative Religion*, trans. Rosemary Sheed (New York: Sheed and Ward, Inc., 1958); and *The Sacred and the Profane*, trans. Willard R. Trask (New York: Harper & Row, 1961). For an inclusive review of Eliade on myth, see Wilson M. Hudson, "Eliade's Contribution to the Study of Myth," *Tire Shrinker to Dragster*, Publications of the Texas Folklore Society, XXXIV (Austin, 1968), 219-241.

2. These are the categories set up by Margaret Rose Sadler, "The Mythological Orientation of John Steinbeck," Thesis University of Texas, 1965.

3. *The Winter of Our Discontent* (New York: Viking Press, 1961), p. 220.

4. Pp. 261-262.

5. P. 44.

6. P. 54.

7. P. 94.

8. P. 52.

9. P. 144.

10. P. 173.

The Railroad
In American Folk Song,
1865-1920

By ANN MILLER CARPENTER

T HE impact of
the railroad on American culture can be partially illustrated by the
appearance of the railroad as the subject of folk songs, especially
during the sixty years following the Civil War. The influence of the
railroad is visible in many different varieties of music among the
common people: hero ballads, protest songs, hammer songs, hobo
tunes, convict songs, blues, and spirituals. No comprehensive bibli-
ography or collection of railroad songs has been published, but the
available materials are numerous. To limit the subject to a workable
size, I have been forced to include only those songs that explicitly
mention the railroad, thus omitting many hobo songs and work
songs that might in some less direct way be associated with railroading. In addition, I have usually limited this study to folk songs
that meet the traditional requirements of oral transmission, con-
tinuity, and variation (see Lawless, 5-6), and I have tried to note
when I have included art songs or popular songs that have become
folk songs to some degree. The volume of railroad folk songs is one
indication of the railroad's impact and influence on music, which
the collector Alan Lomax describes in this way: "No subject, not
even the little dogie, has produced so much good American music
as the railroad. . ." (LA, 406).

At first, railroad songs were in many ways protest songs. The hero ballads, probably the most famous of the railroad folk songs, often depict man pitting his skill and strength against the machine, usually losing his life in proving his need to assert his mastery. The social protest songs of the Irish, the unions, the farmers, and others feature the railroad as an element that in some manner infringes upon basic human rights because of the greed of the railroad bosses. In the songs that can be traced with any certainty to the earlier years, only occasionally is the train pictured in a really favorable manner, perhaps as the object of adoration of some engineer or the symbol of emancipation for the workers. Gradually, however, the railroad is assimilated into the rhythms and performances of the music and becomes more and more a variously interpreted symbol itself, a symbol of man's distant longings, hopes, fears, and regrets.

The hero ballads are the most widely known of the railroad folk songs. They fall into three general groups of attitudes concerning the machine: those that show man's direct challenge of the machine, and those that picture man's heroic actions in times of crisis associated with the machine, and those that tell of men who are admired because they attack or defy the machine in some way. These ballads have in common a hero who is the victim of the machine and who usually dies in attempting to master it. The speed and power of the train are the two elements that are most often mentioned as being dangerous and fatal to man.

The John Henry ballads are probably the best-known songs of protest against the coming of the machine and inevitable technological unemployment. The John Henry tradition has been the subject of numerous studies, and the versions of John Henry ballads, work songs, and related songs number in the hundreds. The two book-length investigations (Johnson, Chappell) of this tradition make a good case for the belief that John Henry was a living man who worked as a steel driver (a man who strikes a steel drill with a hammer to make a hole into which an explosive can be inserted). Evidence seems to support the hypothesis that John Henry worked on the Big Bend Tunnel construction from 1870 to 1872 on the Chesapeake and Ohio Railroad in West Virginia. Officially called the Great Bend Tunnel, it was one of the last large tunnels to be made by hand-drilling. The experimental steam drill was beginning to be introduced in the 1870's, and most studies of John Henry emphasize that contests with steam drills were common during this time.

While the numerous versions of the John Henry songs vary greatly in details, such as the name of the wife, the weight of the hammer, and the circumstances of the wager, the central theme is that of man versus machine. In the background of the song can be seen the scorn and fear of the workers for the steam drill that threatens their livelihood: "Lordy, Lord, why did you send that steam?/ It's caused de boss man to run me, run me like a oxyen team" (Johnson, 73). John Henry, a powerful steel driver, enters a contest with a steam drill, beats the machine, but dies then or soon after. Usually he is said to have made a fourteen-foot hole while the steam drill finished only nine feet (Chappell, 108). He becomes a martyr in the songs as he gives his life to prove man's superiority over a machine. The songs celebrate his brute strength and his determination, especially in the repeated vow, "I'll beat it to th' bottom or I'll die" (Johnson, 93). His death is an inspiration to his fellow workers, just as it has been to all men who feel the need to assert man's mastery of the machine: "If I could hammer like John Henry,/ Lawd, I'd be a man" (Johnson, 82).

Many folk songs celebrate the heroic actions of railroad men in times of crisis, almost all of these songs being based upon actual men and events in the last half of the nineteenth century when railroad disasters became a national disgrace. (See Holbrook, 275-288, on disasters.) Casey Jones, whose name has become synonymous with the term "locomotive engineer," died in a train wreck near Vaughan, Mississippi, on April 30, 1900, and he has become the most famous of the heroes of railroad wrecks. (For background on Casey Jones, see Holbrook, 429-430; Hubbard, 5-23.) An Illinois Central engineer, John Luther Jones (1864-1900) took the name Casey from his boyhood town of Cayce, Kentucky. He had three distinctive characteristics that are now legend: devotion to his engine, a desire to maintain schedules, and a distinctive type of locomotive whistle. On the night of April 30, 1900, he and his fireman Sim Webb doubled over for a sick engineer on the McQueen Ten-wheeler No. 382. They had to make up for a late start, and a freight train at Vaughan failed to clear the track. Casey stayed at his post, plowed into the caboose and two other freight cars, and was the only one that died. According to legend, one of Casey's friends was a Negro named Wallace Saunders who worked in the Canton roundhouse, and it was he who began the first Casey Jones song, which was revised by professional song writers T. Lawrence Siebert and Eddie Newton to become a best-seller in 1903.

The Casey Jones folk songs celebrate his distinctive whistle trademark, his devotion to duty, and his dedication to a schedule. The long, plaintive wail of his whistle had endeared him to all those who listened to the sounds of the trains: "The switchmen knew by the engine moan/ That the man at the throttle was Casey Jones" (Sandburg, 367). In a way, perhaps, the whistle was a symbol of his mastery of his engine, his humanizing of the machine. It was the regimentation, the slavery to time, that partially contributed to Casey's tragedy. As a good engineer, Casey was dedicated to keeping a schedule: "For I'm going to run her till she leaves the rail/ Or make it on time with the southbound mail" (Hubbard, 18). Casey Jones, then, became a symbol of heroic man as victim of the machine. The didactic ending of the folk song pointed out the effects of the machine on man: "Headaches and backaches and all kinds of pain/ Are not apart from a railroad train" (Sandburg, 368).

The Casey Jones song may stem from several earlier pieces, such as "Jay Gould's Daughter," "Been on the Cholly So Long," "Mama, Have You Heard the News," and "Joseph Mica" (Sandburg, 365, 369; Scarborough, 250). Each of these songs involves a good engineer who is trying to maintain a schedule; in most cases the end is a wreck. None of these heroes, however, such as Charley Snyder and Joseph Mica, have the stature given Casey Jones in his song. Casey gives up his life to control the machine, and in this way he prevents further loss of life. Other engineers are unable to avert deaths and injuries of passengers, and they are criticized for their roles in the accidents. Joseph Mickle, the engineer in "Been on the Cholly So Long," is blamed for the injuries on his train and receives no praise for his part in the wreck: "Some were crippled and some were lame,/ And the six-wheel driver had to bear the blame" (Sandburg, 365).

Numerous other wreck songs have been inspired by actual tragedies. "The Wreck of the Old 97," a classic second only to "Casey

Jones," was probably started by David Graves George, who was present at the scene of the tragedy when Engineer Joseph A. (Steve) Broady's train leaped the rails on September 27, 1903, between Monroe and Spencer, West Virginia (Holbrook, 430-432). The element of time, the slavery to a schedule, and resultant excessive speed again contribute to the downfall of the hero who has orders to "put her in Spencer on time" (Botkin, 449). As his train jumped the track, "his whistle broke into a scream," and he was found "in the wreck with his hand on the throttle" (Botkin, 450). Time and speed seem to be the two elements of railroading that are particularly hazardous for man as he attempts to master the machine. (See Cottrell, 2-3, 59, 77.)

Mass tragedies are often eulogized in song, although songs of many deaths have not become as popular as those celebrating the death of a single hero. "Engineer Rigg" is inspired by the wreck of a Negro excursion when a drawbridge is not in place (White, 220). "The Wreck of the C & O" arises from the accident to engineer George Alley's train in 1890 as a result of a landslide (Botkin, 451-454). "The Chatsworth Wreck" tells of the tragedy in 1887 when a burning bridge resulted in the death of eighty-two people who were on an excursion trip to Niagara Falls (Hubbard, 157-166). A snowstorm contributes to the derailing of a train in "The Wreck on the Somerset Road" (L3, 254-256). (In addition to L3, for backgrounds of these wrecks see White, 220; Botkin, 451, 454; Hubbard, 157, 166.) Mass tragedies seem to have resulted from accidents of man or nature (drawbridge, landslide, burning bridge, snowstorm), but still the folk songs emphasize the machine's part, the railroading fanaticism with time and speed, and the heroism of the men who pit their skills against the machine. The railroad is directly blamed for the deaths: "Many a man's been murdered by the railroad" (Botkin, 451). The engine is "like a mad and angry bull" or at best is an indifferent and unfeeling cause of catastrophe. People from all over the country come to look on the dead heroes and to give honors to the men "who the flame and fury fought" (Botkin, 454; Hubbard, 166).

The heroes of railroad songs are not always engineers and not always men. In "The Little Red Caboose Behind the Train," the old conductor has lost his wife on their honeymoon in a train wreck that came about from excessive speed combined with weather conditions (Botkin, 455-456). Despite antagonism between railroad men and hoboes, "Only a Bum" celebrates a hobo who is killed as he warns the train of a burning bridge ahead (Milburn, 134-135). Several songs record the heroism of "Kate Shelley," a fifteen-year-old girl who crossed the Des Moines River railroad bridge during a raging storm in 1881 to warn an approaching passenger train and to save the lives of those in a train that had already plunged into the river (Hubbard, 134-146). About the only heroine or hero that was created by the railroad owners for advertisement was Phoebe Snow, a dainty young lady presented to the public in 1904 to publicize the Delaware, Lackawanna & Western Railroad; the purpose was to convince the public that the service was luxuriously clean because the Lackawanna engines burned anthracite instead of more grimy bituminous coal: "Phoebe Snow, dressed in white/ Rides the road of Anthracite" (Hubbard, 39-40). The Phoebe Snow songs, however, never achieved the popularity and circulation of the true folk songs, which were based on man's most terrified vision of what the railroad can mean to society: the awesome loss of life in wrecks and the human courage admired in times of crisis.

Not all subjects of railroad songs are ideal heroes. Some are actually villains who achieve at least a degree of awe or admiration in the common people by the courage with which they defy the railroad. The most famous of these is Railroad Bill, probably a Negro named Morris Slater who defied the peonage system in the turpentine plantations of Alabama and took to a life of breaking in boxcars and selling the goods (LA, 557). He killed two lawmen before he was cut down in ambush in 1896. There needs to be a comprehensive study of the Railroad Bill songs and legends because many folk song collectors seem unaware of any probable historical parallel. In the many versions of "Railroad Bill," the villain-hero is pictured as something like a runaway engine in that he rides down anything in his path. The verses are short and proceed with rapid action. Railroad Bill never works, he steals all the women, he takes all he can from the farmers, and he is stirred up by corn whiskey to shoot the lights out of the brakeman's hand (Sandburg, 384-385; Work, 240; OJ1, 198-203). He is like the railroad engine in times when it seems to act up for no reason to cause death and destruction. Railroad Bill is celebrated much for the same reason that Jesse James is immortalized as a hero (Sandburg, 375, 420). Both rob and kill, but at the same time, they defy the system and acquire a certain heroic stature in doing so.

Some of the early ill effects of the railroads became suitable materials for folk songs, particularly for those arising from Irish immigrant labor, farmers, unionists, and Negro laborers. Probably the earliest of these railroad songs were those of the Irish immigrants, who arrived in America in masses between 1840 and 1860 to work at man-killing jobs with wages as low as 50¢ a day; much of the surplus Irish labor was siphoned off into Western railroad building (Greenway, 39-42). "Poor Paddy Works on the Railway" reveals conditions of the worker as he curses the luck that brought him to work on the railway. The "Yankee clerk" cheats him in the boss's store, he lacks sufficient clothing, and his wife's death turns him to drinking whiskey. The most vivid passage is probably this description of living conditions:

> And when Pat lays him down to sleep,
> The wiry bugs around him creep,
> And divil a bit can poor Pat sleep,
> While he works on the railway.
>
> (Botkin, 438-439;
Greenway, 42-43)

"Way Out in Idaho" records another case of "the trials and tribulations of a godless railroad man"; here the railroad bosses are certain that the worker has no money and so must remain in virtual slavery or else bum his way back to civilization (Botkin, 440). Somewhat the same tone is set in an Irish lullaby, "Sh-Ta-Rah-Dah-Dey," which records that "times is mighty hard" (Sandburg, 36-37). Although it is a composed song (by Charles Connolly and Thomas Casey in 1888), "Drill, Ye Tarriers, Drill" became almost a theme song among the Irish-American railroad workers during the last years of the century; it records the boss's tyrannical character in a humorous manner as he docks a driller's pay for the time he is blown up in the air during a premature explosion (Botkin, 442-443). The boss's desire to get the job done is emphasized in "Jerry

Go and Ile That Car" (Sandburg, 360; Botkin, 441-442). "O'Shaugnnessy" is yet another ballad of the Irishman's unhappy brush with the railroad (Holbrook, 437).

The farmers had a particular grievance with the railroads, which came to be synonymous with greed as far as they were concerned. The railroad made the farmer dependent on shipping grain by rail, and the adjusted rates became more and more intolerable. This grievance was a principal factor in the Populist movement during the last quarter of the nineteenth century. Didactic songs of the People's Party include stabs at the greed of the railroad:

> The railroads and party bosses
> Together did sweetly agree;
> And they thought there would be little trouble
> In working a hayseed like me.
> (Greenway, 60)

Others who would agree with this view of the greed of the railroad include the would-be gold miner in the Black Hills who advises that "Railroad speculators their pockets you'll fill/ By taking a trip to those dreary Black Hills" (Sandburg, 265). The mountaineer of Kentucky similarly resents the intrusion of the railroad upon his peaceful domain: "I don't like no railroad man/ Railroad man he'll kill you if he can" (Sandburg, 326).

Railroad laborers also felt the effects of the railroad industry's greed as wages declined through the seventies and eighties despite tremendous prosperity for the industrialists. The result was bitter labor disputes, such as the Freight Handlers' Strike in 1882, the Pullman Strike in 1894, and the Southern Pacific strike in 1910 (Greenway, 52-56, 186-187). The Union songs of the time emphasize that "Field, Jay Gould and Vanderbilt" made their millions by treating men like slaves on starvation wages ("The Freight Handlers' Strike," Greenway, 53). Efforts of the striking laborers brought few results because of the use of strike breakers (scabs) and the use of injunction from the government to break the strike, such as in the Pullman Strike in which all American Railway Union members were blacklisted. The laborer's hatred of scabs is plainly seen in Joe Hill's version of "Casey Jones, the Union Scab," c. 1910; Casey appears as a strike-breaker who goes to Heaven only to be sent to Hell by "The Angels' Union Number 23" (Greenway, 186).

Another example of railroad greed was the practice of inducing Negroes to migrate West for permanent work; actually the laborers were given the poorest of treatment with insufficient food and no money with which to return home. Pathetic longing for home, then, naturally occurs in these Negro laborers' songs, such as "Thought I Heard That K.C. Whistle Blow" (OJ1, 220-221). Here the Negro wishes for a train to carry him back home and curses the engineer who brought him away (OJ1, 169). At times, the laborer imagines that some of his friends have come to see him: "I believe my woman's on that train" (OJ1, 222). Many times the laborer decides to return home by any means he can find: "I'm boun' to go hom if I have to ride de rod" (OJ1, 223).

The Negro laborers that worked on the railroad had many songs. On one hand, these songs protest the wretchedness of the working conditions. In other cases, however, the fascination of the train begins to appear, particularly in the wish to work on the train as Pullman porter, conductor, or engineer. Sometimes the Negro expresses the desire to be like the train.

In a survey of the work songs of the Negro gang laborers on the railroad, the most interesting are those that grow directly out of the worker's job and that show his attitudes to his captain, his partner, his hammer, his work, and his pay. The laborer is suspicious of his captain and is anxious that he should not work overtime: "Don' let yo' watch run down, Cap'n" (Sandburg, 370). He emphasizes that he is not going to be exploited: "Yo take Shine's money, but you can't take mine" (Odum, 118). He objects to the cold winters (Sandburg, 458), to winds that "blew up the railroad track" (Sandburg, 379), to working in the mud (Sandburg, 370), and to working in the heat that "hangs around your head till your mind nearly fails" ("Mike," L1, 23). He feels his pride hurt at times (Botkin, 445) and vows to run away if he is mistreated (Sandburg, 139). He wishes that he could get more wages, which are variously described as ten cents a day or forty cents a day (White, 266), and he says that sometimes the pay is withheld altogether (Work, 245). He likes to point songs toward the Captain, as "Cap'n don't like me" (Botkin, 445) or "Cap'n, you look mo' lack farmer/

Than dam' railroad man" (Odum, 118). Yet he always takes pride in his work and likes to brag about his prowess as a workman: "Dere ain't no hammah/ Ina this old mountain,/ Shina like mine" ("My Old Hammah," Sandburg, 458).

At the same time that the Negro laborer protests the conditions under which he works, he looks upon the railroad train itself with fascination: "Darkey, take your hat off when the train goes past" (L1, 41-42). Maybe he enjoys working on the railroad because it offers him a sense of immediate means of escape. He likes to describe the longest trains he has seen (White, 274; LA, 541), and he admires the engine's freedom and speed so much that he wishes he were himself a train: "If I had wings like that engine, I could run an' fly" (OJ2, 93). The train is the way to freedom from any oppression (OJ2, 102), and the laborer imaginatively pictures riding a train or better yet working on the train. He loves to ride on the train so much that he will ride the coal car just to get to go (White, 386), or he will risk being "cracked" on the head to ride even a small train on a short track, the so-called "Dummy Line" (Scarborough, 244). He despises the fact that Negroes are often denied privileges of riding even a freight train, and he wishes that he owned a train: "I'm Gonna Have Ma a Red Ball All My Own" (OJ2, 132). Working on the train seems to be the ideal occupation. The Pullman porter in his handsome uniform is described as a hero who has "pocket full o' money,/ Stomach full o' feed" (OJ2, 186-187). Even more highly praised is the Negro engineer, as in "Reuben." Negroes were not permitted to drive engines on Southern railroads but did work as engineers during the Northern occupation. Reuben was one of these Negro engineers who lost his job when the troops went back north (LA, 566). His whistle became famous among Southern laborers: "You could hear that whistle blow a hundred miles." For the Negro laborer, then, the greatest dream was to run the engine:

> I could pull the bell,
> I could blow the whistle,
> I could pull the bell,
> An' let the engine run.
> (OJ2, 93)

Among the numerous protest songs and hero ballads appear some songs that applaud the coming of the railroad and that show the romance that was associated with the trains and their engineers. After the hero ballads, it is a relatively easy transition to songs like "A Railroader for Me," in which the railroad man takes the place of honor as a romantic figure that formerly belonged to the sailor, cowboy, and lumberjack: "I'd rather marry an engineer/ That wears a striped shirt" (Botkin, 465). Somewhat different, however, are the songs like "The Railroad Cars Are Coming" and "She'll Be Comin' Round the Mountain." These songs celebrate the actual train. There is jubilation at the coming of the transcontinental railway across domains formerly reserved to the prairie dog, rattlesnake, and owl (Sandburg, 358-359). In fact, communities watch for the arrival of the train and meet it with celebrations (Sandburg, 372-373). At the same time that the railroad speculators' greed incurred the wrath of laborers and farmers, new associations and connotations were being developed about the railroad. The railroad was becoming a symbol of freedom, an escape from current woes, and a means of uniting a vast continent.

It is perhaps a sign that the railroad is becoming assimilated into popular culture as the train becomes more and more a symbol in folk songs. One of the most striking symbolic uses of the railroad is made in the late nineteenth and early twentieth centuries in both Negro and white spirituals. The old idea of life as a journey to eternity takes on new imagery as the gospel train becomes the mode of transportation in place of older means such as Jacob's ladder, the chariot, or the ship of Zion. The inevitability of death is suggested in the recurring image of "Same Train" that comes back day after day for different members of the family (J & J, II, 60-62). There is only one train and one track to Heaven (LA, 486), and no difference is made between rich and poor ("Git on Board, Little Chillen," J & J, I, 126-127). While there is plenty of room for everyone, only those who have a ticket (which may be the desire to be saved, baptism, or other things) can be assured of a seat ("You Better Git Yo' Ticket, OJ1, 113). Jesus is usually the captain (OJ2, 202) or the conductor (White, 65), while the crew consists of "Moses and Noah and Abraham and all the prophets, too" (OJ1, 114). Certain undesirables are excluded from the gospel train:

gamblers, jokers, ramblers, cigarette smokers ("This Train," LA, 484). More train imagery comes in the songs with the whistle blowing, cars rumbling on the track, and the train "strainin' eb'ry nerve" around the many curves (OJ1, 114; also White, 64, 65).

Most white spiritual songs that mention the railroad follow along the same lines as the Negro spirituals. In "The Beulah Railway" descriptions of the cars are given, and station, tickets, and baggage are allegorized (White, 422-423). Sometimes the Bible is the engineer, and repentance is the station, as in "The Railroad to Heaven" (Belden, 468). Other closely associated songs are "Oh Be Ready When the Train Comes In" and white versions of "The Gospel Train" (White, 441-442). "Life is Like a Mountain Railroad" has each man as his own engineer:

> Round the bend, and through the tunnel
> Never falter, never fail;
> Keep your hand upon the throttle,
> And your eye upon the rail.
> (Greenway, 16)

Several versions of "The Little Black Train" and "The Funeral Train" picture the train as death, and the passengers have their places reserved for its uncertain schedule by their actions in life (White, 65; Scarborough, 260-261). In one version, "The Little Black Train" has only one small baggage car because passengers won't need material goods at the judgment bar (L3, 46-47). "The Funeral Train" pictures tearful passengers on a train "creped in black," but unlike actual trains, the funeral train has neither whistle nor bell since it approaches the unsuspecting sinner without warning (Scarborough, 262). "The Influenza Train" is associated with these death railroads, since those that leave on the influenza train never come back (White, 424). In a related song, "The White House Blues," the Cannonball Express blows at every station to tell of McKinley's death (L3, 256-258).

The railroad is sometimes described in terms of other known values when it is pictured as a horse, mule, or angry bull (Sandburg, 326), or when it is associated with death or illness. In a much broader realm of folk song, however, the railroad becomes a symbol of man's innate longings, perhaps for freedom or travel, or as the Freudians might say, a return to the womb. In other songs, men look at the railroad as their regrets, a symbol of their wandering since the loss of Paradise and a symbol of dreams that were never realized or things and people left behind.

The train is a sign of freedom in such songs as the abolition tune "Get Off the Track" and the industrial emancipation song "The Workingman's Train" (Greenway, 87). After the Civil War, the Negro continues to see the train as a way to freedom, such as in "Abe Lincoln Freed the Nigger" and "I Went to Atlanta" (Greenway, 102, 126). For convicts, too, the sound of the railroad whistle symbolizes freedom, especially in such songs as "The Midnight Special" (Sandburg, 26, 27, 217). The train often means an escape from present ills, a hope to find better things in a new and distant place. The mystery and suggestiveness of the train is equated with an epic adventure. The appeal of the train to a man is well expressed in this early blues:

> When a woman blue, when a woman blue,
> She hang her little head and cry
> When a man get blue
> He grab a railroad train and ride.
> (Sandburg, 236)

The same admiration for the railroad develops the cherished railroad fantasy of the ghost train running through space and time without end. "The Wabash Cannon Ball," according to one version, is a mythical train that runs everywhere and that travels so fast that the engine takes off into the stratosphere (Botkin, 462). "The Phantom Drag" is another ghost train and has Casey Jones as engineer (Holbrook, 440-441).

The railroad plays a decided role in hobo songs as the train represents the freedom and variety of life valued by hobos whether they are seeking escape from labor or simply from systems of conventional life. (For an account of the hobo and his life, see Anderson. For hobo songs, see Milburn.) Although no actual figures can be established, many authorities believe that from ten to fifty tramps were on every freight train at the turn of the century; these hobos caused expense to the railroad, and thus there developed much an-

tagonism between railroad men and the hoboes. The hobo expresses the antagonism in this way: "Any kind of railroad man to me is
a pain in the neck" (Botkin, 461). Hoboes believed that "Jay
Gould's Daughter" wanted to leave them only the most dangerous
places to ride—the slender rod between the cross section and axle
of the four-wheel truck: "If ride they must, let 'em ride the rod"
(Milburn, 251). No matter what the method of riding (the rods, the
tops of cars, the "blind" or space of baggage car when connected
to the locomotive tender), the hobo's life is precarious and con-
stantly in danger (Milburn, 31). The hobo often has deep resentment toward the conventional society from which he is an outcast,
as he satirically calls himself "the enemy of mankind" (Milburn,
120-121). Despite the hobo's resentment of railroad men and conventional society, he is lured by the train and fascinated by it. He
makes a song to the sounds of the trucks clicking over the rail joints,
as in "The Song of the Wheels" (Milburn, 271-272). The poignant
summons of the train whistle always lures him to the road again even
if he tries to settle down: "There's magic in its mournful wail" (Milburn, 203-205). Most hoboes vow to keep on wandering all of their
lives (Milburn, 169), and they may even wish to view death as one
last ride on the train, such as in "The Hobo's Last Ride," "The Dying
Hobo," or "The Hobo's Last Lament" (Milburn, 41, 131-133, 67-
68, 74-75). Older hoboes lure younger boys to the wandering life
with attractive visions of the road, such as those in "Big Rock Candy
Mountain" (L2, 281). For the hobo, in general, the railroad is a
symbol of freedom as it is the means to the free life that he desires.

Man's attempts to escape present ills do not always succeed, and
for many the railroad symbolizes broken dreams and regrets. At
times, the train is the cruel enginery of fate, separating man from
his loved ones and home. The train whistle may make a man hang
his head and cry because it serves as a reminder of the home he left
behind, as in "Dat Sunshine Special" (Sandburg, 247) and "990
Miles" (Botkin, 464). Even the sight of a train can be a reminder of
all a man has lost, as in "Ten Thousand Miles Away from Home"
(Sandburg, 457). While not responsible directly for misfortune, the
railroad is at least an unfeeling observer of grief. In many blues
songs, the train is the vehicle of melancholy yearning toward things
that are lost and irretrievable.

It is into the twentieth century when at last the railroad appears in songs as an image that is altogether unrelated to the function of transportation. For example, a man snores like "a locomotive engine" (White, 222), a man tells more lies than "cross-ties on the railroad" (Sandburg, 245), and a man without his woman feels like "an engine, ain't got no drivin' wheel" (LA, 587-588). There is some discernible movement from songs of protest against the railroad's excesses, especially the greed of the speculators, to songs of a time when the railroad becomes a symbol because of its transportation function and then becomes an image in songs for other qualities that it possesses.

No study of the impact of the railroad on folk song can be complete without at least a comment on its effect on the rhythms of the music and performances of the musicians. It is easy to see how the railroad work songs are adapted to the specific job concerned. In fact, work songs are usually encouraged by bosses to keep workers in unison, such as "Steel Laying Holler," "Tie-Shuffling Chant," and "Tie Tamping Chant" (L1, 10-12, 14-17, 17-19). The rhythms of the songs coordinate the movements of the workers so that the men become like a machine themselves, whether unloading rails, lining or straightening railroad track, or packing gravel around a tie. It is only one more step from coordinating song to work movements to coordinating song to train movements. The most obvious impact of the railroad on music can be seen in the songs that attempt to imitate the sounds of the moving train—whistles, bells, coasting down-grade, laboring up-grade, and all the rest. Some musicians are especially prized for their ability to give highly musical imitations of the train, especially the train whistles; the record of "The Train" by Chub Parham, *Folk Music of the United States*, Record No. AAFS 10, is an example of a virtuoso performance of this type. Specialists in railroad music often note the deep impression that the railroad has made on popular music, especially jazz and blues. Alan Lomax describes the blues as "half-African and half-locomotive rhythm" (LA, 406). Archie Green, while editing the most recent Library of Congress album of railroad songs, notes the connections between the rail narrative songs and the blues (Green, 4). While pointing out the French, African, and Spanish influences on blues and jazz, B. A. Botkin and Alvin Harlow emphasize the strong influence of the railroad on American music:

. . . in our estimation, the distinctive feeling of American hot music comes from the railroad. In the minds and hearts of the people it is the surge and thunder of the steam engine, the ripple of the wheels along the tracks, and the shrill minor-keyed whistles that have colored this new American folk music. (Botkin, p. 437)

The far-reaching influence of the railroad on American music is an indication of the train's impact on Americans and its gradual assimilation into popular culture.

BIBLIOGRAPHY AND ABBREVIATIONS

Anderson. Anderson, Nels. *The Hobo: The Sociology of the Homeless Man.* Chicago: The University of Chicago Press, 1923.

Belden, H.M. *Ballads and Songs Collected by the Missouri Folk-Lore Society.* The University of Missouri Studies, XV (January, 1940).

Botkin. Botkin, B. A., and Alvin F. Harlow. *A Treasury of Railroad Folklore: The Stories, Tall Tales, Traditions, Ballads and Songs of the American Railroad Man.* New York: Bonanza Books, 1953.

Chappell. Chappell, Louis W. John Henry: *A Folk-Lore Study.* Jena, Germany: Walter Biedermann, 1933.

Cottrell. Cottrell, W. Fred. *The Railroader.* Stanford, California: Stanford University Press, 1940.

Green. Green, Archie. "Preface to *Railroad Songs and Ballads.*" Washington, D. C.: Library of Congress, n.d.

Greenway. Greenway, John. *American Folksongs of Protest.* New York: A. S. Barnes and Company, 1953.

Holbrook. Holbrook, Stewart. *The Story of American Railroads.* New York: Crown Publishers, 1947.

Hubbard. Hubbard, Freeman. *Railroad Avenue: Great Stories and Legends of American Railroading.* New York: McGraw-Hill Book Company, Inc., 1945.

Johnson. Johnson, Guy B. *John Henry: Tracking Down a Negro Legend.* Chapel Hill: The University of North Carolina Press, 1929.

J & J. Johnson, James Weldon, and J. Rosamond Johnson. *The Books of American Negro Spirituals.* New York: Viking Press, 1947. 2 vols. in 1.

Lawless. Lawless, Ray M. *Folksingers and Folksongs in America*. New York: Duell, Sloan and Pearce, 1965.

LA. Lomax, Alan. *The Folk Songs of North America*. New York: Doubleday and Company, Inc., 1960.

L1. Lomax, John, and Alan Lomax. *American Ballads and Folk Songs*. New York: Macmillan, 1935.

L2. ———. *Folk Song U.S.A.* New York: Duell, Sloan and Pearce, 1947.

L3. ———. *Our Singing Country*. New York: Macmillan, 1941.

Milburn. Milburn, George. *The Hobo's Horn Book: A Repertory for a Gutter Jongleur*. New York: Ives Washburn, 1930.

Odum. Odum, Howard W. *Rainbow Round My Shoulder: The Blue Trail of Black Ulysses*. Indianapolis: Bobbs-Merrill Company, 1928.

OJ1. Odum, Howard W., and Guy B. Johnson. *The Negro and His Songs: A Study of Typical Negro Songs in the South*. Hatsboro, Pennsylvania: Folklore Associates, Inc., 1964.

OJ2. ———. *Negro Workaday Songs*. Chapel Hill: The University of North Carolina Press, 1926.

Sandburg. Sandburg, Carl. *The American Songbag*. New York: Harcourt, Brace and Company, 1927.

Scarborough. Scarborough, Dorothy. *On the Trail of Negro Folk-Songs*. Hatsboro, Pennsylvania: Folklore Associates, Inc., 1963.

White. White, Newman I. *American Negro Folk-Songs*. Hatsboro, Pennsylvania: Folklore Associates, Inc., 1965.

Work. Work, John W. *American Negro Songs*. New York: Howell, Soskin, and Company, 1940.

The Professor
Who Didn't Get His Grades In:
A Traveling Anecdote

By JAMES T. BRATCHER

IN the coffee lounge of Sul Ross State College in the fall of 1966 I was told of a professor, a specialist in educational psychology, who was no longer on the faculty. The man had gone to pieces. His wife had left him; and although he was reputed to be a good teacher well liked by students, he had become troubled and embittered to the point of incompetence. On the last day of finals he started hitting the bottle with abandon. The three-day period for turning in grade reports elapsed. The dean, unable to locate the man at his home, finally reached him at a disreputable bar across the tracks. Since the drunk professor had no grades prepared, the dean attempted to read his class rolls to him and secure the grades in that manner. The effort proved useless, however, and the dean was forced to make some disposition of the grades himself, since the best response he could get to his calling off of the names was comments of the order, "That bitch? Give her a D!" or, "Hell, flunk ol' Gibson, the bastard!"

The story was the more interesting to me because I had heard, or rather read, a similar account. In the Spring 1962 issue of *Southwest Review* J. Frank Dobie writes on Douglas Branch, then seven years dead. Branch was an early student of Dobie's and a youth marked for literary achievement; Dobie reluctantly uses the word "genius." By the time he was thirty, Branch had written and published four books, among them *The Cowboy and His Interpreters* and *The Running of the Buffalo*. (In 1926 Branch contributed an article, "Buffalo Lore and Boudin Blanc," to a volume of the Society's Publications.) Before he was fifty, however, alcohol and Skid Row claimed him. The chronicle is a familiar one and toward the close of it, when Fortune's wheel is about to come full cycle, Dobie quotes the testimony of one who knew Branch at Center College, Kentucky, during the academic year 1946-47. I reproduce what is represented as the "common talk" about Branch at Center College, as no doubt it was. Dobie's informant was Mr. John Hakac, now at the University of Arizona.

That year I was taking Freshman English under a couple of jackasses at Center. Dr. Branch had the maturest and brightest students in a Shakespeare course. He was a celebrated campus character . . . .

Dr. Branch was living alone in one room. According to student belief, his wife had died in a fire and his resultant suffering was so great that he took to the bottle and lived in utter loneliness.

The end of the semester (1947) came and Branch had not turned in his final grades. The deadline passed and still no grades were in. I'm just telling what was common talk. The college dean went to Branch's room and knocked on the door. He got no answer, walked in anyhow, and found Dr. Branch drunk in bed. Rousing him slightly, he asked if the final grades were ready. Dr. Branch said no. "Get up and get these grades. We need them," the dean admonished. Branch remained supine. The dean now suggested that he would read the class roll and Branch could say off A, B, C, D, etc., as an estimated grade. Branch agreed. Most of the class were GI's. Finally the dean came to a Mr. Smith. "I can't recall that name at all," Branch said. The dean identified Mr. Smith in some way. "Oh, yes," Branch cried, "I remember him now. Give him an A—poor devil, he's married."

Just recently I again met with the story—this time in Edmund Gosse's collection of literary sketches, *Critical Kit-Kats* (London, 1896). It has the same pattern as the other two stories. It concerns Walter Pater, who was not drunk but merely languid and had no wife to cause him grief.

Pater showed much tact and good sense in his attitude towards the college life. He lectured rarely, I believe, in later years; in the old days he was an assiduous tutor. His temperament, it is true, sometimes made it difficult to work with him. On one occasion, at the examination for scholarships, he undertook to look over the English essays; when the examiners met to compare marks, Pater had none. He explained, with languor, "They did not much impress me." As something had to be done, he was asked to endeavour to recall such impressions as he had formed; to stimulate his memory, the names were read out in alphabetical order. Pater shook his head mournfully as each was pronounced, murmering dreamily, "I do not recall him," "He did not strike me," and so on. At last the reader came to the name of Sanctuary, on which Pater's face lit up, and he said, "Yes; I remember; I liked his name."

The anecdote of the professor who failed to submit grades falls within the framework of what J. Barre Toelken, in a forward-looking article reprinted in Jan Harold Brunvand's *The Study of American Folklore* (New York, 1968), has called "The Folklore of Academe." "Professor" stories must be as old as Socrates. As a matter of fact, a number of passages in Plato's *Dialogues* show Socrates to have had some typical "professorial" characteristics such as becoming so lost in thought or disputation as to be insensitive to heat or cold and the passage of time. Suppose that Socrates had had to give exams and furnish grade reports on initiates in the cave. What couldn't Aristophanes have made of this? He might have produced the first instance of the story of the professor who didn't get his grades in. Here is Socrates, suspended in his basket (as in *The Clouds*) and in meditation, forgetful of his overdue grades. He is metaphorically drunk on ideas. His wife Xantippe is troublesome, but she is not the cause of this kind of drunkenness. All that is lacking is someone to enact the role of the grade-seeking dean.

My guess is that the first professor to attract or incur the modern story of the gradeless professor "took his tods," to use Artemus Ward's phrase for overdrinking. In two of the versions that we have examined the cause for drink is the professor's wife, who has left him or died tragically. Here is the element of pathos dear to popular imagination. In the story about Pater there is no wife because Pater had none and because his well-known immersion in art is sufficient to explain why he had no marks for the students. The Pater version nevertheless follows the same pattern as the other two. The general situation is the same, the roll is called, and in the end the teacher recollects a student for a humorous reason. There must be many stories with this pattern on widely scattered campuses.

THE PROFESSOR WHO DIDN'T GET HIS GRADES IN : 123

Unequivocal Justice

By J. T. McCULLEN, Jr.

AS early as 1533, "Pantagruel persuaded Panurge to seek counsel of a fool."[1] As late as 1966, John W. Wade cited a legal altercation which was resolved by an idiot. Pantagruel was a man capable of settling controversies which, in jurisprudence, were "about as clear as Old High German." He not only shamed the great law professors of his day (experts from the Sorbonne and Padua), but also achieved recognition as one whose "judgment was reputed more marvelous than Solomon's."[2] Rabelais emphasizes the following query made by Pantagruel: "Since Panurge had found no true satisfaction in the answers of specialists, why did he not consult some lunatic?"[3] John W. Wade is Dean of the School of Law at Vanderbilt University. Even so, he did not hesitate to include among decisions recorded in the highest federal and state courts of America an example of unequivocal justice rendered by "a very natural Fool, and such a notorious Idiot as in all Paris his like was not to be found."[4]

What Pantagruel and Dean Wade have in common is knowledge of a folk motif which is no less notable for its timelessness than for its ubiquity: an imaginary payment for an imaginary obligation or debt. To read criticism of present-day courts is to realize that the expert's search for justice is a timeless, perhaps a fruitless, quest. Tracing Anglo-American court procedures to the medieval trial by combat, David Dressler says that today, instead of fighting with lethal weapons, the accuser and the accused fight by proxy: their attorneys. "The jury decides which 'side' fought the better fight. But fight it is and the object is to win, not necessarily to reveal the truth." The appearance of this motif in tales from various countries attests to its universality. The objective of this paper is to demonstrate that the simple wisdom of the folk can achieve unequivocal justice, no matter how long procedures of sophisticated courts remain as unsatisfactory and "as unscientific as an appendectomy performed with a tomahawk."[5]

Although Rabelais is the author who has most influenced the circulation of a major version of the tale cited by Dean Wade, a fifteenth-century manuscript entitled the *Nouvelles de Sens* predates the Pantagruel version.[6] The story relates how a porter held bread over vapors emanating from a roasting goose. The cook said nothing until the porter had wolfed down his last mouthful, but then demanded payment for the smoke of the roasting meat. Though the porter replied that he had in no way damaged the meat, the cook reminded him that one does not roast geese to feed riffraff for nothing and threatened to knock out his teeth. The porter, in turn, asked whether the cook would let some passerby render a decision in the case. At hand was John the lunatic, who listened to the argument and then asked the porter to hand over a coin. Ringing the coin several times on a counter, John the lunatic announced the following decision: "That the porter who ate his bread by the smoke of the roast has duly paid the cook with the jingle of his money." Observers asked "whether a more logical and judicious settlement could have been made by the Parliament of Paris, the Rota of Rome, or the Areopagites of Athens."[7]

This particular motif, which Stith Thompson labels *Payment with the clink of the money* (J1172.2), exists in oral and written versions dispersed from India to America. Whereas Thompson lists references which have to do only with food, to search for recurrence of the motif is to discover that it is sometimes related to two other sources of possible obligations or indebtedness: work and sex.

Natives of and visitors to various countries have given me versions of payment with the clink of a coin for the aroma of food. Ibrahim Natto of Mecca says that tales of beggars sued for holding bread in fumes rising from shish kebab but acquitted for the clink of their coins are common lore in Saudi Arabia. Gloria Kelso of Arlington, Virginia, reports that she has heard similar tales narrated in Iran. Students from India, Lebanon, Syria, Jordan, and Egypt have added versions, the particulars of which differ primarily because of the individuality of the narrator. Ulrich Boehnke of Germany says that he not only grew up hearing this basic story, but also studied with a Berlin professor of law who cited an example of justice rendered by the clink of a coin when a man was sued for holding bread over a skillet of frying chicken.

A Turkish version of this motif merits attention because, like Pantagruel, the narrator shifts emphasis from beggar and cook to the judge: Nasreddin Khoja, the comic folk hero of Turkey. After a poor man had held crusts of bread over a saucepan until the bread became soft enough to satisfy his appetite, the cook hailed him into a court over which the Khoja presided. Shaking two coins from his own pocket, the Khoja addressed the cook: "Now listen to this. . . . All the satisfaction you will get will be the sound of these coins." Amazed at the decision, the cook exclaimed, "But, your Honour, what a way to treat me!" "No," said the Khoja. "It is perfectly just settlement of the claim. A man who is so mean as to ask for payment for the steam of his meat will get the sound of these coins and nothing more."[8]

Certain variations in tales which associate the clink-of-the-coin motif with food are noteworthy. One modification, which is traceable from the seventeenth through the twentieth centuries, depicts the accused as one who does not hold bread over a spit or pan, but who merely sniffs aromas which pervade a general area. "Whether a man may live some time, or how long, by the steam of meat, I cannot tell," says Sir William Temple in a health treatise written during the late seventeenth century; "but the justice was great in that story of a cook, who observing a man to use it often in his shop, and asking money because he confessed to save his dinner by it, was adjudged to be paid by the clinking of a coin."[9] A fully developed version of the story of a man prosecuted for standing by a restaurant door and breathing aromas which lured paying customers inside is included in a currently popular anthology of French literature. [10] The case cited by Dean Wade narrates the experience of a beggar who, smelling odors issuing from a house, decided to devour a piece of bread while sniffing the smell coming from the kitchen. ". . . his Sense was so delighted with the fresh smell of the Cook's Meat, that tho' he did not lay his Lips to any Morsel thereof, yet in the end his Stomach was so well satisfied with the smell thereof, that he plainly acknowledged to have gotten as good a Breakfast, as if he had eaten his Belly full of the best Chear." The enraged cook learned something of justice when he agreed to let the next passerby, the most "notorious Idiot" in Paris, settle the dispute. Fool though the judge was, he decreed "that as the poor Man was satisfied with the Smell of the Cook's Meat, so the Cook should be recompensed with the Noise of the poor Man's Money." [11]

An Irish folktale shifts payment for an imaginary debt from the clink to the smell of money. One of six young men ate only soup but was charged for a pound of meat. When he refused to pay for the meat, the waitress confiscated his hat. Walking past the hotel, Daniel O'Connell inquired about the argument and remarked, "If this fellow didn't eat the meat, 'tis strange that he should have to pay for it. Give him back his hat."

"He didn't have to eat it," said the woman. "The smell of my meat filled his belly."

O'Connell took his own hat and threw a fistful of money into it. "Come over here now," he said to the woman. "Place your nose over this money and take your time smelling it. Fill your belly with it." By this means, the accused man recovered his hat. [12]

A second Khoja tale illustrates yet another variation on the clink-of-the-coin motif: a shift from food to work. Demanding a share of money paid to a woodcutter, a plaintiff said to the Khoja: ". . . as he was cutting it I passed by, and each time he drove in the ax I cried, 'Hengh! hengh!' to encourage him." The judge was pleased to test the usefulness of the Khoja, his "Shadow." The Khoja listened and then responded to the plaintiff: "Of course you are right. The idea of his receiving all the money, while you stood by and took so much trouble every time he drove in the ax! It is not to be thought of!"

When the defendant objected that, since he had done all the

work, no one else could justly claim a share of the money for "looking on," the Khoja replied: "Hush, my man, you don't understand." He called for a money tray and dropped the coins, one by one, into it. Then he turned to the woodcutter and said, "Take your money—and as for you [turning to the other], take the sound of the coins as I rung them on that tray, for that is all you will get."[13]

The theme of imaginary payment for imaginary indebtedness associated with work is almost as universal as is the motif linked with food. Many years ago, Jim Brown of Sampson County, North Carolina, used to wander from barn to barn telling tales and thereby earning welcome to whatever farmers ate during nights they sat up to cure their tobacco. He had sawed none of the oak logs and did not hesitate to sit by as a farmer lugged them to his furnace. Looking on, he sometimes told the story of a man who, like the plaintiff of the Khoja tale, demanded a share of the money received for crossties because he had given an encouraging grunt each time the woodsman wielded his broadax. [14]

Physicians of the Renaissance included the clink-of-the-coin motif in discussions of remedies for the lover's malady, a problem well-known to readers of Chaucer and Shakespeare. In 1599, "The Meanes to Cure the Loue Foolish and Melancholiks," by Andreas Laurentius, Physician to the King of France, introduced English readers to the wisdom of relying upon paying with the clink of a coin when two people who make a particular agreement on sex later reach an impasse.[15] Although basic elements of tales narrated by Dr. Laurentius and Dr. James Ferrand (1623) are essentially the same, to reproduce the story told by Dr. Ferrand is appropriate; for an 1842 edition of the *Encyclopaedia Britannica*[16] still recommended his treatise as useful reading for distraught lovers. The story reads as follows:

And sometimes a mere dreame doth the like [cures love madness] : as may appear by that story of a certaine young *Aegyptian*, that was extremely in love with one *Theognis*. . . . This young *Inamorato* prevailed so farre with this wench, that at the last she consented to satisfy his desires, upon condition that hee would give her a certaine summe of Money: which he very readily condescended unto. It fortuned in the meane time, that as this lusty youth one night lay asleep in his bed, hee dream't that he embrac'd in his armes his beloved *Theognis*: and his Fancy was so strong upon him, that hee conceived himselfe to enjoy her really, in the height of Amorous dalliance: and was by this meanes cured of his Malady. Which the Damsell coming to have notice of, she demanded her salary of him: and upon his refusall to pay it, she sues him in a court of Iustice, alleadging for the reason of this her proceeding that she had performed the condition on her part required, in that she had cured him of his disease. Which when the Iudge heard, he commanded the young man, that hee should bring into the Court the summe of money agreed upon betwixt them, and there powre it into a Bason: and withall decreed, that as the *Aegyptian* had contented himselfe with a bare Imaginary Pleasure, conceived in the enjoyment of Her body, in like manner should she bee satisfyed with the sound and colour of his gold.

Though, as Dr. Ferrand adds, the damsel objected that, whereas the dream had quenched the desire of her lover, the sight of his gold had increased hers all the more, this remedy of the lover's malady is less hazardous than the one which immediately precedes it. *"Diogenes* going one day to the Oracle of *Delphos*, to aske counsell, what was the most soveraigne and speediest Remedy for the cure of his sonne, that was growne mad for Love," Dr. Ferrand reports, "received this answer: 'that he must enjoy Her, that was the cause of his Madness.' " [17]

A different motif whereby the accused makes imaginary payment for an imaginary debt associated with work is common lore in oral traditions of the Middle East. Ibrahim Natto of Mecca and Harold Jam of Iran have given me Arabic and Persian versions which parallel the following Khoja tale entitled "A Suit for Payment of 'Nothing' ":

Two men came before the Judge and pleaded as follows:—
Plaintiff: "Your Honour, this man has a load of wood on his back, and as he was walking along, his foot slipped. He fell, and all the wood came down with him. He begged me to put it on his back again, and I asked him what he would pay me for doing it. He answered, 'Nothing.' I said, 'All right. I agree to do it for nothing,' and I put the wood on his back. I then asked him for payment of 'nothing,' and he will not give it me. Your Honour, I demand my rights. Let him pay me 'nothing' here and now."
The Judge always handed over delicate questions like this to our friend the Khoja, who, having listened attentively, said, "Your claim is just. He must keep his word. He shall pay."
Then pointing to the rug on the divan, he said to the claimant, "Just lift that rug a bit and tell me what is under it."

The man looked and answered, "Nothing."

"Why," said he, "that is what you want. Take it and go."18

The three tales referred to differ only in certain details. The Arabian judge told a plaintiff to look into an empty drawer, and the Persian judge ordered a claimant to run his hand under a mattress.

A Balochi tale, which emphasizes the injustice of imputing indebtedness to a man endowed with an active imagination, supplies still another variation upon the theme of unequivocal justice. In response to a royal decree that any man who stood a winter's night in a river would win the hand of a princess in marriage, one man submitted to the test and survived. When the king asked why he was still alive, though all other men who had stood in the river had frozen and died, the survivor answered, "A fire was burning on the hillside, I kept my heart fixed on the fire, and so I came out alive." After accusing the man of having warmed himself by the fire, the king dismissed him and ordered the princess to prepare food for her father. "My Lord the King!" she informed him, "the griddle is on the house-top, and the fire is in the yard; as soon as the griddle heats I will cook your food." Admitting that the suitor could no more have warmed himself by the fire on the hillside than the griddle could heat itself by fire in the yard, the king acknowledged the error of his accusation and permitted the suitor to be married to the princess.19

Lore of Italy and Germany shifts imaginary payment for an imaginary obligation to confession and absolution of sin. Bandello tells how a penitent who had been abused by a friar invited him and his subordinates to an imaginary banquet. When the hungry friars complained because the dishes were empty, the penitent repeated what their superior had said while refusing to absolve him for wishing to kill an enemy: "The thought is as good as the deed."20 Pauli records a similar tale. When a penitent confessed that he once desired to kill a man, a priest replied, "You have to go to Rome for the killing, or you must give me four florins to be absolved. For I have the Pope's power over forty persons, and you need my aid." When the poor man retorted that he had killed no one, but only intended to do so, the priest answered, "God takes the volition for the deed." Aware that he was trapped, the penitent agreed to give the money demanded, if the priest would first absolve him.

Once absolved, however, he gave only the regular confessional penny. In response to demands for the sum agreed upon, the penitent said, "Take the volition for the deed! I intended to give you the four florins." 21

Final variations on means whereby unequivocal justice is rendered emphasize payments made with shadows cast upon bodies of water and images in mirrors. In *Courtiers' Trifles*, Walter Map tells the story of a tyrannic king who heard that a young man had dreamed of holding his queen in an intimate embrace. When the youth confessed his dream, a wise judge reminded him that the penalty for violating the queen was to give the king a thousand cows. The judge then pronounced the following sentence: "that the young man shall place his thousand cows in the sight of the king in a line on the bank of Lake Bethenium, in the sunlight, when the shadow of each cow may be seen in the water, and that the shadows shall belong to the king, but the cows to their former owner, since a dream is but the shadow of reality."22

Tales of women who, having dreamed of intercourse with men, demanded payment for services rendered are even more common. A folktale of India illustrates how they were paid. There was a harlot who had developed the habit of fleecing whatever man appeared in her dreams. When she dreamed of a Brahman, she dispatched her servants to seize him and extort payment for enjoying her favors. Deeply troubled, the Brahman appealed to his king. The king assured the woman that she would be paid, if she would wait a few moments. "He accordingly caused a post to be fixed in the street and the sum tied to the hem of a garment and suspended from the top of the pole. He then placed a mirror underneath . . . and told the woman to put her hand into the mirror and receive the money." When she objected that to do so was impossible, the king replied: "As the Brahman appeared to you only in a dream, you may take the money that appears in the mirror."23

Inasmuch as either rendering or receiving unequivocal justice is a subject of timeless interest, it might be rewarding to conclude with an account of a recent trial the ambiguities of which contrast with the infallibility of the motif under discussion. "In one case, the advocate found just what he needed to defend his client, a North Carolinian who had fired across the state line and killed a man in Tennessee," David Dressler reports. "When North Carolina attempted to charge him, the attorney cried foul. The act, he pointed out, was completed in Tennessee, and the law requires a man to be tried where the act was completed. North Carolina had to agree. Tennessee then tried to extradite the killer as a fugitive from justice. Impossible, the counsel fumed. Since his client had never been in Tennessee, how could he be a fugitive from that state?"24

NOTES

1. *Gargantua and Pantagruel*, tr. Jacques LeClercq (New York, 1936), p. 430.

2. *Ibid.*, pp. 201-202.

3. *Ibid.*, pp. 430-431.

4. *Cases and Materials on Restitution*, second edition (Brooklyn, 1966), p. 224.

5. "Trial by Combat in American Courts," *Harper's Magazine*, CXXII (April 1961), 31.

6. F. C. Perry, "The Classification of Narrative Motifs Apparent in *The Legende de Maister Pierre Faifeu* and in the *Nouvelles de Sens*," a Master's thesis, University of South Carolina, 1941, p. 63.

7. *Gargantua and Pantagruel*, p. 433.

8. *The Khoja: Tales of Nasr-ed-Din*, ed. Henry D. Burnham (New York, 1924), p. 22.

9. *The Works of Sir William Temple* (London, 1770), III, 287-288.

10. "Le Pauvre et le Rotisseur," *Promenades en France*, ed. René Belle and Andrée Hass (New York, 1951), pp. 16-17.

11. *Cases and Materials on Restitution*, p. 224.

12. *Folktales of Ireland*, ed. and translated by Sean O'Sullivan (Chicago, 1966), p. 234.

13. *The Khoja*, p. 74.

14. Memory of observations by the author.

15. *A Discourse of the Preservation of the Sight: of Melancholike Diseases; of Rheumes, and Old Age* (London, 1599), p. 122.

16. George Coffin Taylor, "Love Is a Wonderful Thing Department," *New Yorker*, XXII (Feb. 22, 1947), 87-88.

17. *A Treatise Discoursing of the Essence, Symptomes, Prognosticks, and Cure of Love or Erotique Melancholy* (London, 1640), pp. 273-276.

18. *The Khoja*, pp. 76-77.

19. M. Longworth, "The Balochi Tales," *Folk-Lore*, III (1892), 519-520.

20. *The Novels of Matteo Bandello* (London, 1890), VI, 208 ff.

21. Johannes Pauli, *Schimpf und Ernst*, ed. Johannes Bolte (Berlin, 1924), II, 298. The translation is mine.

22. *De Nugis Curialium, or Courtiers' Trifles*, trans. Frederick Tupper and Marbury B. Ogle (London, 1924), p. 115.

23. "Miscellanea," *Indian Antiquary*, XXVI (1897), 27-28.

24. "Trial by Combat in American Courts," p. 33.

Marriage Customs
In Thessaly & Macedonia

By PINA S. STURDIVANT

I. KOKKINOS PYROGOS IN THESSALY

MRS.
Efthemia Stamos, about eighty (she was not sure), from the Thessalian village of Kokkinos Pyrogos, gave the following account of the wedding engagements and practices of her village as they were observed in her girlhood. According to her, many of the customs have disappeared completely, although some are extant today in a modified form. Customs did vary somewhat from village to village.

On the evening of April 30, May Day Eve, the young unmarried girls of the village went in procession to the river, each carrying a garland of white flowers in the center of which was fastened her mother's wedding ring. The flowers from the garlands were thrown into the river one by one while the girls sang a song which included each girl's name. This ritual brought luck in obtaining a husband. Before returning to the village, each girl broke a switch from a tree growing by the river and twisted it around her waist to ward off pain during the rest of the year.

When a boy or girl of Kokkinos Pyrogos reached marriageable age the parents and relatives, who arranged the engagement, paid

135

close attention at festivities, church, and public gatherings to the young people. "Ah, there is a beautiful girl. She would grace the house of our son." "That boy will work in the town, and his wife will not have to go to the fields." "His father owns large fields and many animals, so the woman he weds will not go hungry." Thus went the discussions. Once the parents had decided upon a likely prospect, emissaries, usually relatives, were sent to the parents of the choice and dickering began in earnest. The bride-price[1] was one of the most important items discussed.

The full week before a wedding, which usually took place on Sunday afternoon, was filled with preparations and festivities. On Monday invitations to the wedding were sent by word of mouth to the relatives in the village and by packets of sugared almonds to those outside the village. The bride-to-be chose her *vlamsas*, helpers, unmarried girls, usually close relatives; and the groom-to-be chose his *flamades*, male helpers. Both vlamsas and flamades were presented with half-aprons which were worn during the entire week to indicate their status.

The vlamsas went to the bride's house on Monday and on each subsequent day of the week, where they busied themselves sewing on items for the *pricka*, the linens furnished by the bride, and doing other work pertinent to the wedding. The girls sang, told jokes, and made a gay time of it. One of their tasks was to make a red-colored dough and place it around each of the bride's fingers, singing a ritual song throughout the procedure. The dough remained all night on the girl's fingers, and when it was removed the following morning, her fingers were dyed red for the wedding.

On Saturday morning two small boys were sent around the village with a jug of wine to invite all the people of the village to the wedding.

During the day, the bridegroom sent two flamades, led by musicians playing the tune for the "giving of the mirror" and bearing a looking glass for the bride so that she could look her best on the following day. The bride did not immediately answer the summons to the door but let the musicians play for a while, sometimes as much as an hour, to prove that she was begged for. After the presentation of the mirror, the two flamades danced in front of the house, and before leaving they stole something from the bride's father, such as a chicken. The "stolen" item was returned after the wedding, or, in some cases, given to the newlyweds.

On Saturday night the bride and groom celebrated separately in their own homes with their relatives and special friends, who brought presents. At the bride's a close relative, usually a sister, gave something sweet to each guest, who then danced to whatever tune the musicians were playing. After the arrival of all the guests, the Dance of the Vlamsas was presented, the vlamsas dressed in their aprons and dancing in a line led by the bride. During the party at the groom's, ouzo, an anis-flavored liqueur, was passed to the guests by one of the flamades, everyone drinking from the same glass; wine and food were also served by the vlamsas and flamades, but only the men ate or drank until the serving of the main feast. The bride left her party early and went to a house somewhere else to sleep in order to be fresh and pretty for her wedding day. The party itself lasted until dawn the following morning.

On Sunday morning the groom was shaved by a barber who came to his house. Guests threw money into the shaving water to pay the barber's fee.

The groom sent a horse and cart to the bride's home to collect the pricka. His flamades, who were responsible for the chore, pounded on the door and demanded the pricka, but the bride's vlamsas, keeping the door blocked, demurred, saying, "Give us some money." The flamades gave them a few coins, and the pricka was removed to the new couple's home, almost always the home of the groom's family, with whom the newly wed couple would live.[2]

When it was time for the wedding, the groom, preceded by the musicians, first went to the house of his *kombara* (similar to a godfather, but a hereditary position passed from father to son to grandson, etc.), and with him walked to the church, where they waited at the door for the arrival of the bride.[3]

If the bride was from another village, the boys from the groom's community mounted their horses and raced to her village as soon as the groom and his kombara left for the journey. The first boy to arrive and greet the bride was presented with a jug of wine to be taken to the approaching groom to speed his way along the road and with a coat as a gift for himself. The second and third-place riders were also given coats.

Before the wedding, the bride was dressed with great ceremony in the traditional wedding dress of the village by her vlamsas and by the firstborn boy of her family.[4] The boy put on her first shoe to assure that the first child would be a boy. He also helped her put on her dress in order that she would have many male children. Finally, the bride herself put on her jewelry, consisting of silver belts, bracelets, and necklaces, in a special sequence, singing ritual songs under her breath as she did so.

Into the bride's clothes was placed a hazelnut filled with mercury and sealed with wax. After the wedding the hazelnut was swallowed whole. It had to be found after its passage through the body, cleaned, and kept as a good-luck charm, protection against witchcraft and the evil eye. Failure to find the nut might presage sterility or early widowhood.

As the bride left the house, her mother gave her a glass of wine, which she drank before throwing the glass to the ground to break it, thereby breaking her tie to the house to prevent having to return to it again except as a guest. The failure of the glass to break was an omen of ill luck.

The bride, following the musicians, went to the church, her father walking on one side, her oldest brother on the other, the rest of the family behind them, throwing rice, a symbol of fertility, over the bride so that she and her husband might be blessed with as many children and as many years together as the grains of rice.

At the church door, the bride bowed three times to the groom and kissed his hand to show her subservience, and he handed her a bouquet of flowers. The kombara provided and placed on their heads the white crowns to be exchanged during the ceremony, crossing them from the head of one to the other until the ribbons were completely entwined; he also provided a piece of new white material which he pinned to the backs of the bride and groom before they entered the church to hold them together. (The bride later made either a coat or a dress from the material.)

The couple went together into the church and bowed three times to the priest. During the service when it was mentioned that woman is subservient to man, if the bride quickly placed her foot over the groom's foot, she cancelled that part of the ceremony. The wedding rings of both the bride and groom, which had been worn on their left hands during the engagement, were removed from their fingers by the priest and the kombara, who, making the sign of the cross, transferred them to the couple's right hands.

At the end of the wedding ceremony, the kombara placed his hands on the shoulders of the bride and groom and jumped, throwing his weight on them, making a wish that they be blessed with five boys. Relatives of the couple struck the kombara on the back until he had repeated this ritual three times.

People threw rice and almonds, both of which signified fertility and longevity, over the couple as they left the church, preceded by the musicians, and marched to the home of the man's mother, where they would now live.[5] The groom's mother met them at the door and gave each a piece of candied fruit. After they had eaten it, she threw a length of lightweight cloth around the couple, retaining hold of the ends, and drew them into the house together over a bar of iron placed on the doorsill which the newlyweds had to step on simultaneously as they entered, in order to secure a marriage as strong as iron; the crossing of the sill was done very carefully, right feet first, for bad luck was sure to follow if either stumbled. The piece of cloth was a symbolic tie to hold them together forever and was later made into a blouse by the bride.

The relatives of the groom followed the couple into the house and gave money to the bride. She, in turn, gave them presents, usually clothing. After the exchange, the kombara danced, holding his gifts in his hands, followed in sequence by the relatives, also holding their presents, and by the vlamsas and flamades. The groom then danced with either the bride or the kombara. Finally, the bride danced alone to a special song which went in part, "This is our bride, she walks like a duck." (This song was a humorous jibe at the traditional wedding dress of the village, a skirt full at the top but tight at the ankles, which made walking difficult.)

A virgin boy and girl made a wedding loaf, the girl spreading the flour through an upside-down sieve over a kneading trough while the boy poured the water, the two together kneading the dough. When the loaf was ready, the bride and groom discussed aloud where to put this first bread of their life: "If we throw it on the roof the mice will eat it and we will fight like mice; if we throw it in the pen the pigs will eat it and we will fight like pigs; if we throw it in the field the dogs will eat it and we will fight like dogs." Eventually, they took the loaf and secreted it somewhere, never revealing its hiding place.

The bride and groom then danced on a small handwoven mat of wild iris, the guests standing in a circle around them holding sticks with which to strike the couple's toes or heels if they stepped off the mat.

On Monday morning following the wedding, the bedclothes and the bride's gown were hung on a line or thrown onto the ground outside the door to show that the bride had been a virgin. Had she not been, she was expelled from the house, by which act the wedding was effectively annulled.

During the morning, the bride took a large apple and stuffed it with coins. All the relatives went to the river in a procession led by musicians and the bride, who threw the apple into the water. The boys of the families dived for the apple, and he who retrieved it kept it and the money. Neighbors came to the house during the day, bringing cakes and fruit, and all ate and danced together.

At least once in the full year following the wedding, each household of close relatives came bringing cake and candied fruit as an invitation to the couple to a feast, always a bounteous one. When the couple departed from a feast, the bride was presented a plate with almonds, a rose, and occasionally an orange on it. These feasts were to make the first child strong—there was sure to be one on the way by then.

II. MELISSOHORI IN MACEDONIA

From the Macedonian village of Melissohori came the following folk customs, as told by Mrs. Krisula Ziakis, a thirty-year-old matron living in the household of her mother-in-law and her grandmother-in-law, as is still customary. Mrs. Ziakis gave the following information about the superstitions and wedding rites that existed during her own girlhood, adding that the same procedures had been followed in the time of her mother and of her mother's mother.

Since the time of Eve woman has worried over the problem of how to acquire a man and how to make sure she captivates the right one. In Macedonia, as elsewhere, practices and methods for accomplishing these goals have been developed and transmitted by word of mouth down through the ages.

Girls of Macedonian Greece are given three chances during the year to discover, through supernatural aid, the man who is destined to be their lifelong protector.

The first occurs on St. Theodore's Day, which falls on the first Saturday in Lent of the Greek Orthodox calendar. Any young lady may go to the church and receive from the priest some grains of cooked wheat. She then places the wheat under her pillow, saying:

> St. Theodore,
> You who roam in the woods
> And meet fortunes,
> Find mine and reveal it to me.

That night, if she dreams of a man that man will become her husband. However, in the event that no dream occurs, she may repeat the procedure two more nights. If at the end of the third night she has had no revelation, the poor girl must resign herself to the lamentable fact that there is no man in her future.

A second opportunity for discovering one's true love is provided on St. John's Day in June by a procedure known as "potluck," which is participated in by all the village maidens. A large pot is set in the village square and filled with water from all the different fountains of the village. The water is called "dumb water" because the girls may not speak during the process. When the pot is full, each girl drops in some token which is specifically hers: a ring, earring, or bracelet. Finally, each girl blindly fishes out a token and takes a mouthful of water from the pot. Holding the water in her mouth, she draws a paper on which a verse is written, and which, in conjunction with the token, has prophetic significance. The verses are found in and copied from the back of a Greek almanac or calendar. Still constrained to silence, still holding the dumb water in her mouth, each girl carries her token and the paper on which the verse is written to a crossroad, sits, and listens. The first name that she hears spoken will be the name of her future husband.[6]

A third and final chance to discover the man in a maiden's life comes at the end of August, on St. Phanourios' Day. St. Phanourios

(*phanourios* means "I reveal") is the patron saint of maidens. On this day a special cake, known as *phanouropita*, made of cinnamon, oil, flour, and soda, is taken to the church where it is blessed by the priest. The cake is then cut into small squares and a piece given each girl. The square is taken home and placed under the girl's pillow. As with St. Theodore's cooked wheat, the charm has three nights in which to work. Woe betide the girl who fails to conjure a vision during this last opportunity of the year!

The arrangement between families of Macedonian villages for the engagement of their children was similar to that of the Thessalians.[7] A matchmaker was appointed by the two families to serve as a go-between for the settlement of the amount of the pricka. When the matchmaker had concluded the engagement agreement, the boy went to his prospective bride's house and presented her with a round gold coin called a *simadhi* as a sign they would get married. He also gave her jewelry, clothes, and cosmetics, and he bought a present for everyone in her immediate family. The girl, in return, gave presents to the boy and to all members of his family; also, she bought a new pair of shoes for the matchmaker because, ostensibly, he wore out his shoes going to and fro making arrangements.

A large majority of the weddings took place in the month of October because the men were not working in the fields during that month.

On Thursday preceding the wedding loaves of bread were made by young girls and one elderly woman who had borne many boys, her participation insuring that the new couple would have many children, preferably male. Singing as they kneaded the dough, the bread-making group formed it into loaves and placed it in the oven that every house had in its yard. One of the songs they sang went, in part:

> The oven is burning,
> It is shining. . . .
> The handkerchief of our bridegroom
> And the kerchief of the bride.

The round wedding loaves, called *klikia*, were made with the standard bread recipe but were decorated with sesame seed; and two special loaves, one for the bride and one for the groom, were garnished with honey or sugar so that their life together would be sweet. It was imperative that everyone who attended the wedding party eat some of the bread.

The young single girls who were special friends of the bride took the trousseau of the bride to her home-to-be and set up the new household for her. The bride herself could not see the house before her wedding, for to do so would cause bad luck.

On Saturday morning before the wedding, an invitational committee, including a drummer and a pipe player, went about the village with a *klondiri*, a special bottle full of wine, and small round loaves of bread for the people invited. The animals for the wedding feasts were slaughtered and prepared for cooking on the same morning, the musicians playing throughout the process.

Sometime during the afternoon, the groom sent to the bride an emissary, accompanied by musicians, with a large basket holding a dress, underwear, and shoes. The girls then washed her hair, singing a ritual song, before dressing her in the new clothes for the party to be given in her home for all the relatives and friends of both families. At about eight o'clock in the evening the groom sent a pan filled with cooked food—bread, rice, meat, and fish—and the wedding ring to the bride, who ate every bite of the food and placed the wedding ring on her left hand, where it remained until its transfer to the right hand during the wedding ceremony. The guests began arriving, each congratulating her and giving her a wedding gift of money. The party, which lasted all night, was under way. As with her Thessalian counterpart, the bride left early, going to the house of friends in order to get a good night's sleep.

Sunday, at noon, the groom went to the barber for a shave. His friends followed him, teased him, and sang songs about his approaching wedding while the barber attended to him.

The bride dressed with the help of young single girls, who used incense and bay leaves to make her clothes smell sweet. The girls sang many songs as they helped the bride dress. Here is part of one:

> My bride, angels embroidered your dress
> And on the left side painted your mate.
>
> Our bride is young,
> She is well brought up,

She has had no
Trouble or sorrows.

Today the sky is white,
Today the day is white,
Today the eagle
Marries the pigeon.

I will sing for the man's eyes
That chose this girl.

The bride wrote the names of all her single girl friends on the soles of her shoes. The girls would marry soon whose names had been erased by the end of the wedding procession when the couple entered their home. After all that walking, it would be rare indeed if any name had not been worn off.

As the bride left the house, she said, "Mother, water my flowers. I am going away." She carried a tall cross covered with gold paper and two apples also covered with gold paper, a symbol of many harvests, from the door of her house to the church door, where she kissed the hand of the best man, who then gave her a gold coin. The bride carried no flowers and was given none—flowers were for funerals.

As with the Thessalian weddings, the bride could avoid subservience to her husband by stepping on his foot at the appropriate point in the ceremony. At the completion of the ceremony, rice was thrown at the couple in the church to establish roots for them.

The wedding party then danced in the village square before continuing to the home of the groom's mother, where the newly wed couple would live. Before entering the house, the couple took a loaf of bread, broke it in two, and threw the pieces into the house ahead of them to bring prosperity. The bride stepped into her new home with the right foot first to avoid bad luck. Once in her new home, she gave a present to each of the groom's relatives.

The groom took a cat by the back legs and tore it into two pieces to show his supremacy over the household. Although this particular practice is not often followed today, it has given rise to a Greek saying, "He should tear the cat," used in reference to a man whose wife is a termagant.

At the wedding reception held in the new couple's home following the wedding, there was a large cake decorated with many multi-colored silk ribbons, one end of each embedded in the icing and the other end arranged at the side of the cake, the group forming a circle around it. At the end of one of the ribbons was tied a gold ring, hidden in the icing. All the single girls present took the outer end of a ribbon, and all pulled together. The girl who had the ribbon with the gold ring attached would be the next to get married.[8] The reception lasted all night. During the early morning hours of Monday, some of the guests, supposedly drunk, went to the house of relatives and stole chickens, which they carried to the newlyweds.

On Monday morning the bride's gown was thrown outside the door, just as in Thessaly. Relatives and friends came by all during the day bringing sweets, usually candied fruit, for the couple. On Tuesday morning following the wedding, the bride went to the village fountain and carried water to the house, and that evening she and her husband made a round of all the relatives of both, visiting each family briefly. The couple were invited to a feast at the home of the best man on the Saturday following the wedding, and to a feast at the home of the bridesmaid the following Sunday.

When Christmas of the wedding year came, the couple was invited to dinner at the house of a relative on each of the fifteen holidays of Christmas. On Christmas day the couples married during that year returned to the village and danced in the village square (dressed in village costume during Mrs. Ziakis' mother's time, but in regular "Sunday best" today), all the people of the village coming out to watch and to choose the most handsome couple of the year.

NOTES

1.   In modern Greece, the bride-price no longer exists, and the pricka, once merely a collection of handwoven and embroidered linens done by the girl herself, has become a "husband-price," or dowry, which may consist of money, land, goods, or even a job (the girl's ability to support the family), presented to the prospective groom, who brings nothing but himself to the marriage. A girl's marriageability goes in direct ratio to the size of her pricka, which may account for the day of mourning declared in the household of some families when a girl baby is born, the sons of the family being forbidden by custom to marry until a suitable dowry is provided for all the daughters of the house.

According to Mrs. Stamos, this reversal in payment or dowry came about after "the great war" (referring to the war with Turkey, 1922, and the subsequent civil war in Greece), probably because so many men were killed and so many others emigrated during that period, leaving far too many single women in ratio to eligible men.

2.   The woman's world was a clearly defined matriarchal one, the bride subject to the orders of her mother-in-law, just as the mother-in-law was subject to the will of her mother-in-law should the older woman still be living, as was frequently the case.

3.   When a wedding took place in the bride's home, as was the practice in the girlhood of Mrs. Stamos' mother, the groom carried the largest apple he could find to the door of her house and threw it over the roof. Small children raced to see who could get the apple first.

4.   Sometimes, should the bride's father or mother be dead, the firstborn of a closely related family whose parents both still lived was chosen to fulfill the office instead to prevent her from becoming a widow.

5.   When the groom was from another village and the bride would be leaving with him after the wedding, there was dancing in the churchyard before the couple left.

6.   Mrs. Ziakis had some doubts as to the efficacy of this charm, it being entirely too easy for mischief-makers to deliberately walk by and call out the name of some homely or elderly man or the name of a boy whom it was known the girl despised.

7.   Perhaps the rather cold-bloodedness of the parents' consideration influencing their choice of a husband for a daughter is what led to the seriousness with which young women took the divinations of St. Theodore's Day, St. John's Day, and St. Phanourios' Day, those supernatural presentiments being the only romantic element involved, and romance being essential to the feminine psyche, the Woman's Lib movement notwithstanding.

8.   In Ilo, Peru, I attended a wedding reception in which this ceremony with the ribbons in the cake was performed. In so far as I was able to ascertain, there was only one Greek family in the town, and the practice there antedated the arrival of that family.

The Johannesburg Mine Dances

By MARTIN STAPLES SHOCKLEY

FROM Houston to Johannesburg I traveled 10,000 miles, but the two cities are in other respects quite close. Like Houston, Johannesburg is a bustling industrial, commercial, financial center of more than a million inhabitants. Like Houston, Johannesburg has a race problem, a crime problem, and a traffic problem. All over South Africa, people in other towns told me with civic pride, "This isn't Johannesburg."

What oil is to Houston, gold is to Johannesburg. Huge deposits of what a Houstonian might call yellow oil lie under the Witwatersrand, the white water ridge which lends its name to the nation's monetary unit, the rand, worth currently $1.40. What Johannesburg has that Houston hasn't is the huge yellow mine dumps, taller than its skyscrapers, bigger than its city blocks, scattered wide around the white water ridge.

South Africa maintains eight universities, four English, four *Afrikaans*. An English-medium University, The Witwatersrand, or "Wits," is located in Johannesburg. I went there to lecture on American literature. Sunday morning we drove out to attend the mine dances. Although identified by John Gunther, who saw them, as "one of the great sights of Africa," these dances were not men-

147

tioned in any of the recent books on Africa which I consulted. I regret that Alan Moorhead did not write about them.

The big gold corporations, mostly owned by the British, use contract labor. Able-bodied Africans are recruited in the protectorates and the reserves, signed up for periods of months or years, and shipped to Johannesburg, where they are housed in corporation compounds. The corporations provide housing, food, medical care, and police protection. Most men live at subsistence level in order to send part of their wages back to feed the families they left behind in the mud huts. The corporations provide for all the needs of their workers, including recreation, which is the stated purpose of the Sunday morning dances.

We drove about fifteen miles out to the Durban Roodepoort Deep, Ltd., where the dances were being held. We were one car in a stream of traffic, winding past the huge yellow dumps, on some of which mine machinery was operating. In and alongside the road, hundreds of black men walked or loitered. In a field near the dance arena, some were playing rugby. Signs directed us to the arena, where mine police manned the parking lots. Ushers passed out programs which identified the participating dance teams by tribal designation and geographical location. The dances were in progress when we arrived. We found good seats downstage center.

The arena is a bowl, perhaps a thousand feet in circumference, enclosing a spacious dirt-floored circle where the dances are performed. The dancers are surrounded by spectators who sit on tiers under a roof. The dance area is open to the sky. Seating arrangements are Jim Crow, with the choice section reserved for "Europeans." A white master of ceremonies puts up signs which announce the dance teams by tribe and program number. A mimeographed program announces, "European visitors are welcome, but the privilege of attending these dances is on the strict understanding that no use is made of the occasion for commercial or publicity purposes. These dances are staged primarily for the recreation and entertainment of the Bantu Mine Workers." (I hereby certify that I have no commercial or publicity purpose. This paper is presented primarily for the recreation and entertainment of the Texas Folklore Society.)

The dance teams enter from one side, exit from the opposite. While one team is leaving, the next is entering. Movement is continuous. For me, the performance consisted of three elements: costume, music, dance.

Costumes were varied and extravagant. All the men wore short white underpants. Usually the musicians and the dancers of each group were costumed differently. Most were barefoot; some wore leg wrappings, below the knees; a few wore red or white undershirts, but most torsos were bare; headdress of skins or feathers was common. There seemed to be a mélange of vestigial tribal costume and miscellaneous articles of civilized clothing. Colors tended to the strong primaries, red, I believe, predominating. Many of the dancers carried shields or spears which were used in the dances. Spears were brandished in movements suggesting threat and menace to an enemy; shields, made of hide and decorated with interlaced strips, were brandished also, but were often used to beat flat against the ground in rhythmic and emphatic punctuation of the dance.

The musicians entered first with their instruments: drums, xylophones, and whistles. Some drums were made of wood, some of metal barrels; all drum heads were of animal skins; some drummers used their hands; some used sticks, either bare or with a head of padded skin. Usually the musicians sang or chanted; sometimes both musicians and dancers whooped together. Some dancers wore tin cans tied below their knees; when they stamped, pebbles in the cans rattled in rhythm.

Movement varied from slow monotony to wild abandon. The most impressive feature was rhythm, now heavy with the drum beat, now weaving intricate variations on the drums. One group danced in gum boots, clomping heavily; another wore bells around their torsos, rippling their chest muscles to produce rhythmical jangling. There were line dances and circle dances, ensembles and solos. The program identified the dancers as Baca, Barotse, Bakwena, Basuto, Swazi, Pondo, Mchopi. In mid-morning there was an intermission, and we went outside for tea and cake, the proceeds to go to Bantu Charities.

Let me say a word about each of three dances. The gum-boot dancers were members of the Baca tribe, coming from the eastern boundary of the Cape Province near the Orange Free State. According to legend the dance originated in a Mission School in Natal about 1900. Because the pupils of the school were forbidden their traditional dances and because they were the only natives who wore shoes, they originated this peculiar stomping dance. Some years later when Zulus working on the Durban docks were issued gumboots, they saw the heavy boots as most appropriate for the stomp. All the dancers wore them, clomping in heavy rhythm to the pounding of the drums as their line of perhaps twenty men wound around the arena. Movement was slow and monotonous. I suspect that this dance may have originated as a satire of the slow, heavy movement which the impediment of shoes imposed upon African youth previously barefoot, fleet, and free. I sensed a tone of mock solemnity, which was, however, frequently overwhelmed by the heavy sensuality of the pounding rhythm.

An entirely different dance was performed by the Amakwenkwe, a Xhosa tribe from the eastern coast of the Cape Province. They were a large group, forty or fifty men, wearing strings of bells tied tightly around their chests, just under the armpits and above the nipples. Some of them also wore tin cans tied just below their knees. They formed a double line behind a leader, and at the command of a whistle began to undulate their chest muscles so that the bells jangled rhythmically. They took short jumping steps. This routine was interrupted by the frenzied stamping of the men who wore the tin cans, the pebbles in the cans making a terrific rattle as they pounded their bare feet on the dirt. They would advance, shake, retreat, in obedience to the whistle. The advancing step is *siyahamba*; the retreating step is *kuhlehla muva*; and the shaking part is *kuteya*. The three movements are as balanced, unified, and harmonious as the movements of a Greek chorus, although, even in *Lysistrata*, I have never seen such enthusiastic sensuality. The whole performance is in high key with frenzied music and movement. It is a ceremonial dance performed by the young men before their initiation.

The most unusual dance was performed by the Amakwaya, who are Christian Shagaans from Mozambique. During the preceding dance, I saw a large black man dressed in white shirt and slacks enter the stands and take a seat near the middle of the Jim Crow section. When the dance began, he stood up and shouted to the dancers, evidently giving directions or commands, and the dancers shouted replies. As the dialogue developed, it was apparent that the dancers were shouting jibes and insults. His commands became vociferous, and their replies more mocking and taunting. I perceived that he was impersonating the white boss and that the dancers were satirizing him. The black audience, who could understand what was being said, was convulsed with glee. They whooped in apprecia- tion as the dancers gesticulated and cavorted to their own devasta- ting repartee. Meanwhile, the mine manager, a tall, well-dressed man, exuding authority like a recently appointed Department Head, watched and listened poker-faced. This performance was the most enthusiastically received of the entire program. In contrast to the gum-boot dance and the bell dance, both of which were line dances whose movements were tightly formal even in frenzy, this repartee dance was performed with what seemed to be complete freedom of movement, each dancer cavorting in the style of his own shouted insult. These dancers created a gorgeous spectacle of spirited defi- ance before yielding the arena to the next group.

White South Africans express varied opinions of these dances: some say they are mere tourist bait, further exploitation of the workers; others say the real purpose is to keep the labor force from thinking about wages, hours, and working conditions. (There are company unions, but collective bargaining is illegal, and the govern- ment administers conditions of employment so as to maintain the choice between semistarvation on the reserves or labor in the mines.) Anthropologists travel thousands of miles through the back country villages to witness in native habitat the originals of which these mine dances are reproductions. Such performances are approved by government policy, which is to promote tribalism as an anti- dote to African nationalism. I heard this policy referred to as "back to the kraal." Unquestionably, there are economic, social, and polit- ical implications in the dances, apart from which I found them a thrilling spectacle of gorgeous barbarism and unrestrained sensuali- ty. I saw them only once.

Having attended a dozen Texas Folklore Society meetings, I re- call during my years no program time devoted to dance. You may recall that volume one of our publications contains an article on Texas play-party songs and dances, volume seventeen one on folk- dance calling, volume nineteen one on rain dancing; but there is not much. Yet dance is a genuine folk art, as valid for our purposes as song or tale. I suspect that we have in our varied folk cultures dances ranging from "London Bridge Is Falling Down" to Comanche war orgies that offer a fertile and comparatively neglected area to Texas folklorists. I see no reason why we should leave this field to anthropologists and professors of P.E. I venture to suggest that some of us might investigate the Negro, Mexican, and Indian dances of Texas. Even Anglos dance. I should enjoy a demonstration, and recommend one for next year's program.

Contributors

JAMES T. BRATCHER is now teaching at the University of Texas at El Paso. He has just concluded an exhaustive index to the Publications of the Texas Folklore Society from the first through the thirty-fourth volume.

JAMES BYRD teaches courses in folklore and literature at East Texas State University in Commerce. In the summer he conducts a week-long conference on folklore which is open to the public.

SARA L. CLARK is a graduate student in English at the University of Texas. Her study of shells as grave decorations began in a seminar conducted by Américo Paredes.

BILL F. FOWLER studied frontier humor under Mody Boatright. He has just completed work for the doctor's degree at the University of Texas. He is in his second year of teaching at Southwest Texas State University.

SYLVIA GRIDER lives in the Texas Panhandle and so knows dust storms by experience. She teaches in Pampa.

JOHN IGO is a teacher of English at San Antonio College. This is his first contribution to our Publications. At the 1971 meeting he read a paper on "guardians," twin animals, urns, or other decorations placed on either side of a doorway or entrance.

KYRA JONES, whose husband Dan teaches at Austin College in Sherman, read her paper on Steinbeck at our 1969 meeting in Dallas. She holds an M.A. from the University of Texas.

E. HUDSON LONG has been active in the affairs of the Society for a number of years. He read his paper on O. Henry at our 1969 meeting. He is chairman of the English department at Baylor University.

ANN MILLER CARPENTER won first prize in our 1969 student contest with her paper on railroad songs, which she wrote in a seminar of Mody Boatright's at the University of Texas. After taking a doctor's degree in 1970, she went to San Angelo College to teach English.

CHARLES B. MARTIN is a member of the English department at North Texas State University. He has made several visits to Spain with his family.

J. T. McCULLEN is a Renaissance specialist, but he is also a productive scholar in the field of folklore. He is professor of English at Texas Technological University.

ESTHER L. MUELLER was born and reared in Fredericksburg. She has taken an active part in movements and organizations devoted to preserving and memorializing local history and customs. As a free-lance writer she has published many articles and stories in newspapers and magazines.

E. J. RISSMANN is well known to readers of our Publications as a writer on the hill country and hill folk. In his "shack" (his word) where he likes to spend the day on a hill southwest of Austin he has collected many artifacts of earlier times. He has the information of a historian and the temperament of a poet.

MARTIN S. SHOCKLEY observed the Johannesburg dances while he was a visiting professor in South Africa. His regular post is at North Texas State University. He spends the summers contemplating the snowy peaks of Estes Park.

PINA S. STURDIVANT, since taking an M.A. at the University of Texas, has made a career of teaching abroad—in Columbia, Venezuela, Greece, and Peru. She was in Greece from August 1966 through June 1968. In obtaining information on marriage customs in Greece she was assisted by interpreters, a granddaughter of one informant and a granddaughter-in-law of the other. At present she is living on her parents' ranch near Matador.

Index